A Disciple's Heart

An Introduction to Opening Your Heart to God

by

William J. Clark, Jr.

with

CH (COL) William J. Clark, Ret.

Keys To Understanding Life Series

A Disciple's Heart
Book 1 of the *Keys To Understanding Life Series*
www.KeysToUnderstandingLife.com
www.ADisciplesHeart.com

Published by
Innovo Publishing, LLC.
www.innovopublishing.com

Copyright © 2009 by William J. Clark, Jr.
All rights reserved.

No part of this publication may be reproduced, stored in a retrieval system or transmitted in any form or by any means electronic, mechanical, photocopying, recording or otherwise, without the prior written permission of the author.

All Scripture taken from the NEW AMERICAN STANDARD BIBLE®, Copyright © 1960, 1962, 1963, 1971, 1972, 1973, 1975, 1977, 1995 by The Lockman Foundation. Used by permission. All rights reserved.

ISBN 13: 978-0-9815403-1-3
ISBN 10: 0-9815403-1-7

Cover Design & Interior Layout: Innovo Publishing, LLC

Printed in the United States of America
U.S. Printing History
First Edition: September 2009

Dedicated with honor

To those who have seen and heard,
To the teachings they have given,
And to those who seek to see and hear.

Praise for *A Disciple's Heart*

"They [the authors] pose honest questions and provide honest answers, never sugar-coating their responses as many religious guides tend to do."

"The authors' complete lessons are not provided in their entirety here; A Disciple's Heart is only one volume {Book One} in the Clarks ' series of lesson plans, titled the "Keys To Understanding Life Series."

- *ForeWord CLARION Review*

The ability to link the true Discipler (the Holy Spirit) with the disciple (the Christian) is unparalleled. As a former missionary in Africa, *A Disciple's Heart* would have truly benefited me had I read it before going. Had I realized the power of the Holy Spirit available to me, I could have been more prepared to find the comfort and strength that I often lacked. *A Disciple's Heart* reminded me it is possible to experience the presence of God on a daily basis, and to encourage believers that they too are not alone.

– Stephen Allen, former missionary to Africa

A Disciple's Heart brings into focus the kind of discipleship that is intentional, purposeful, and available to every believer. Discipleship is not a church program but a process. Three discipleship settings are described which allow the believer to listen and learn from the Spirit of God. The authors encourage the reader to learn how to have daily, direct communication from The Teacher (Spirit of God within). *A Disciple's Heart* will challenge you and intrigue you. Yearning for more? You will see yourself here.

– Dr. Linda Homeyer, Professor of Professional Counseling, Christian Counselor, Director of Adult Education in her church

I have been blessed to be a part of the authors' ministry for almost 2 years. I have experienced significant changes in all areas of my life especially in my relationships, but most importantly in my relationship with God. *A Disciple's Heart* is a gift to those of us who seek a more intimate relationship with God. The significance of discipleship is huge when you are trying to skillfully listen to God! *A Disciple's Heart* gives wonderful examples of how Christians may learn to listen to God in different discipleship environments. It has helped me to understand the difference between being a passive Christian and an active Christian who can interact with the Holy Spirit of God on a day to day basis. It is a life changing experience.

– Kathleen Repa, Real Estate Agent and mother of two

Contents

Acknowledgements 1

Introduction 3

Chapter 1: **The Purpose of Discipleship** 9

— General Characteristics of Discipleship

— What Does It Mean to "Go Beyond the Elementary Teachings of Christ?"

— Discipleship Environments and the Need They Fulfill

— Essentials for Going Beyond the Elementary Teachings of Christ

— A Personal Relationship with God Involves Personal Interaction with His Spirit

— Satan and Our Old Self-Nature Are Involved in the Spiritual War

Chapter 2: **Going Beyond the Elementary Teachings with a Human Teacher** 59

— What Is the Purpose of the Human Teacher?

— Why Is a Personal Relationship with the Human Teacher So Important in This Discipleship Environment?

— How Do We Cultivate Detachment Toward Our Old Selves and Why?

— What Constitutes the Lessons a Disciple Receives from the Human Teacher?

— How Is the Lord's Discipline a Discipleship Lesson?

- Is There a Difference Between Being a Student of Christ and Being a Disciple of Christ?

- How Is Being Discipled by the Human Teacher Different from Being Mentored?

- What Is the Difference Between Christian Counseling and the Human Teacher/Disciple Relationship?

- How Does Preaching Relate to the Human Teacher's Teaching Role?

- What Is Involved in Recognizing a Human Teacher Capable of Discipling Others Beyond The Elementary Teachings of Christ?

- What Are Some Other Characteristics of the Human Teacher Who Disciples?

- What If a Human Teacher Isn't Available and My Church Body Doesn't Have Such a Discipleship Environment?

Chapter 3: **Overview of Fellowship for Discipleship** 123

- Different Kinds of Fellowship for Different Purposes

- Supporting One Another in Relevant, Spiritually Intimate Life Sharing

- An Overview of Satan's Work against a Fellowship for Discipleship

- A Word of Encouragement

References 145

Coming Soon 146

More about *Keys To Understanding Life Series* 150

ACKNOWLEDGEMENTS

There are many to whom we are grateful for being part of our lives, whether in healthy or unhealthy ways, but most of all we are grateful to You, Lord. Through many of our life experiences we have not been able to feel gratitude, but the Lord has taught us how to change our hearts in all things.

It is a challenging walk God calls us to, but we can experience a peace within that is unknown to those who aren't always sure where to step along the way. During the writing we faced some really tough times, but because of the gift of the Spirit of our Lord, our hearts were continually transformed, and we were able to serve God well. We are truly thankful for the gift of being able to interact with God in each challenging situation.

We thank our family for their love, patience and support for us as we wrote and listened to the Spirit of God teaching us how to be thankful, joyful and at peace during times that would have normally been filled with deep sadness! We are deeply grateful to our friends who, during their own busy schedules, were willing to read the manuscript and offer their thoughts and suggestions. We thank our spiritual family, who consistently walks with us, supporting and encouraging us as we seek to do the same for them!

We are grateful to the help and services of Innovo. Their kindness and friendliness has been of great support at precisely the time we needed more of that.

Acknowledgements

It is a high calling to walk with the Lord, and we must seek His voice within to walk well with Him. We acknowledge those readers who share in the thoughts given here; may you let the Lord bless you as you live each day seeking to interact with His Spirit within you.

INTRODUCTION

Opening your heart to God involves working with Him to change what is often in your heart. *A Disciple's Heart* reminds us that the purpose of being discipled is to develop your ability to allow the Lord to change your heart.

In being discipled, we focus on learning to open our hearts to God. We seek to understand and learn the principles and teachings contained within the written Word of God. Developing your heart involves learning by allowing the Spirit of God to speak to you in a variety of ways, including through worship, Bible study, prayer, and your interactions with believers.

A Disciple's Heart reminds us that the purpose of being discipled is to help us change how we live by interacting with the Spirit of God within us. Being discipled is to help us reflect the Lord in the ways we act and interact in the multitude of situations we experience in life. Being discipled is about developing your ability to recognize and follow the Spirit's counsel and guidance in your heart so your actions are an expression of what the Lord would have come from your heart. But when we believe we are to be discipled primarily by gaining Scriptural knowledge and information, it is sometimes easy to assume that we are living as disciples of Christ in our daily affairs. How are you being discipled?

We often view discipleship and being discipled as concepts which describe what happens to us when we do the variety of

Introduction

things we do both in church and in our own devotional or study times. *A Disciple's Heart* examines how the concept of *being discipled* needs to be closer to the foreground of learning to live for Christ. It seeks to make the task of 'being discipled' — opening your heart to the Lord — more tangible, based on how discipleship was demonstrated in the Scriptures. It seeks to reinvigorate our concept of 'being discipled' by placing the spotlight on its relationship to opening our hearts to the voice of the Spirit of Christ within us.

A Disciple's Heart reminds us of the relationship between being discipled and the opening of our hearts. That relationship between being discipled and opening our hearts deals with learning to skillfully experience and exercise an ability to interact with God's Holy Spirit as He seeks to interact with us in various life situations.

In short, A Disciple's Heart looks at the purpose for having the Spirit of the Lord within us--which, in part, is to help us know what the Lord wants us to do in response to the trials of life. A Disciple's Heart seeks to strengthen and encourage those who earnestly want to build continually on that God-given opportunity, with the support of other like-minded believers.

1. **DETAILED PURPOSE OF THIS BOOK:**

    a. To remind us that the "elementary teachings of Christ" (Hebrews 6:1-3) are only the beginning of discipleship that enables us to live well for Christ in real-life situations.

    b. To remind us that in order for discipleship beyond elementary teachings to be effective, a believer must recognize their own need to be discipled.

    c. To examine Scriptural descriptions of the "meat" versus

the "milk" of discipling others, and of being discipled.

d. To refocus on discipleship as including learning how to have skillful personal *interactions* with Christ by interacting with His Spirit, who was given to us.

e. To highlight the importance of the personal interactions and bonds between believers, which are vital to being discipled and learning how to live a life guided by the Spirit.

f. To remind us that one part of what is to make Christians unique are the kinds of bonds and relationships we have.

g. To remind us that another part of what is to make Christians stand out is not just *what* we do (go to church, participate in church programs, etc.), but *how* we respond to stressful, emotional and uncomfortable situations common to all mankind.

h. To highlight , conceptually, the following spiritual skills as being essential to learning to open our hearts and hear the voice of God:

   i. The skill to recognize when Satan is attacking and tempting us.

   ii. The skill to transform emotional pain and stress into peace and love.

   iii. The skill to hear the changes the Spirit seeks to make in us during various life situations.

   iv. The skill to hear the Spirit's instructions and counsel concerning how to act whenever our choices in real-life situations have spiritual implications. In other words, the skill to live the divine nature of God's written Word by interacting with its Author.

Introduction

2. **FOUNDATIONS:**

   a. The Spirit was given to us permanently by the Father as a result of the sacrifice Jesus made on our behalf (Ephesians 1:13-14).

   b. There are basic and elementary teachings from the written Word of God which provide the beginning of discipleship (1 Corinthians 3:1-2).

   c. The Spirit is capable of guiding us into all truth we may need to live well as disciples of Christ (John 14:26).

   d. We are capable of tuning out the Spirit (1 Thessalonians 5:19) such that we may not always hear His guidance and counsel for us as individuals.

   e. Being guided into truth involves being able to transform our hearts during trials (Romans 5:3-5). This transformation skill is vital to avoid quenching the Spirit.

   f. To live for the Lord, we must cultivate the skill of paying attention to our hearts (1 John 3:18-24).

   g. The "fulfillment" of being discipled involves becoming skillful at interacting with the Spirit of God in our hearts (1 John 3:18-24).

   h. Interaction with the Spirit, during real-life situations, facilitates continual learning and the ability to continually pass away the old self (2 Corinthians 5:17) whenever it seeks to assert itself in daily living.

   i. Being guided into truth includes being trained by the Lord, and His discipline is not always pleasant (Hebrews 12:11).

   j. Being able to learn from the Lord's discipline involves learning how to persevere with His guidance and direction (Hebrews 10:36).

k. During real-life situations that require us to learn and persevere, we must have faith in order to be at peace with situations when the outcome is uncertain (Hebrews 11).

l. We need training in handling real-life applications that involve perseverance (Hebrews 10: 36; James 1:2-4). That training goes beyond the elementary teachings of Christ (Hebrews 6:1-3).

3. **RECOMMENDED PREREQUISITES:**

To profit from this book, the only prerequisite is a love for the Lord and a desire to learn more about how to live as His disciple. Some Scripture references are in parenthesis and in the body of the text. They are provided so you may review the Scriptures for yourself; reviewing them is encouraged. However, for the most part, when a Scripture is referenced, the subject of that Scripture is discussed within the text, so you don't have to look it up immediately. Still, taking the time to do so is strongly recommended.

4. **SPECIAL CONSIDERATIONS:**

While this book seeks to provide very useful and practical insights concerning the challenge of living for Christ, it is introductory in nature. This book is the first of a series (described in the back of the book) and emphasizes that discipleship, and being discipled beyond the elementary teachings of Christ, includes cultivating certain spiritual skill sets. **This book does not address the "how to" of the spiritual skills mentioned. The "how to" is a book in its own right** (forthcoming — see "coming soon" in the back of this book).

Introduction

The discussions presented seek to provide readers, who aren't familiar with the "how to" of those skill sets, an appreciation for **why** cultivating them is critical to their spiritual growth.

The book also serves as an encouragement and reminder for those who disciple others to include training on the vital spiritual skills that the Scriptures indicate are part of being discipled and learning to experience God more frequently in everyday life. The book indicates that such training compliments believers' abilities to share Christ with others, and it enhances believers' abilities to demonstrate why it is so practical for new believers to also be discipled.

Finally, though using the terms *skills* and *spiritual skill sets*, this book only seeks to clarify the **concept** that, with God's help, we can become more proficient (be discipled) in doing our part in responding to the voice of the Spirit of God within our hearts.

Skills in interacting with God have both similarities to and differences from "people skills." You can learn to clarify what you think is being said and ask questions. You can identify and minimize things you do which prevent you from hearing well: learn to catch yourself at jumping to conclusions and avoid assuming the worst about someone or some situations.

With people, profitable two-way communication is not entirely up to you; it hinges on their communication skills too. However, God's communication skills and motives are perfect. He makes no mistakes in what He tells you or how. The more you become skilled in your part of being discipled by Him through your heart, the more you will be able to understand and participate in the two-way interaction. We cannot acquire these practical kinds of *spiritual skill sets* without God's help. As you read, remember that *spiritual skills* always involve learning to submit, surrender and transform your heart in Christ.

Chapter 1:
The Purpose of Discipleship

Growth Step 1:

To recognize the goal and purpose of discipleship and to identify the three basic discipleship environments.

Growth Step 2:

To examine what discipleship is supposed to do for your relationship with God.

Growth Step 3:

To understand the five essentials a believer must have to be effectively discipled beyond the elementary teachings of Christ.

Today, many church leaders are very concerned about the health and vitality of the Body of Christ. They are asking important questions. How do we help Christians mature in the faith? How do we revitalize the church? How do we help Christians deal with the difficult realities of everyday life? How do we help Christians walk with the Lord daily when they are at home, at work, and at play? How do we communicate the specific and real-life nature of what God can do and what He wants to do in a believer's life? How do we teach these things to believers, each of whom is a unique individual with different problems, challenges and life circumstances?

The Purpose of Discipleship

Church leaders are not the only ones asking questions; believers in the pews are too:

- "How does my walk with the Lord make my normal, everyday life better?"
- "How does my personal relationship with God help me deal with real-life issues and problems?"
- "How do I feel good about myself and my relationship with God when I'm not at church and am at work or home?"
- "How do I experience God more?"
- "How do I experience God in daily activities?"
- "How does God speak to me?"
- "What comes after salvation?"
- "What does God want me to do, not just generally in life, but in a particular situation?"

At their core, all these questions and issues deal with a person's daily walk with Christ. They deal with issues of the heart. The answers come when we are discipled and learn to skillfully open our hearts to the Lord. So, what is discipleship?

The purpose of discipleship is: *learning how to glorify God by intentionally cultivating your personal relationship with Christ (as His disciple) through the ability to hear His Spirit, who permanently dwells within believers because of Jesus' sacrifice, and who speaks directly to you in your heart, seeking to teach you what is God's will for you both generally through life and specifically in a given situation.*

That is one long sentence. It leaves a lot of room for discussion, and on its own, it really isn't adequate. There are several characteristics about the Scriptures, the Spirit of God, and Satan's intentions which *A Disciple's Heart* holds to be true. Let's look at them briefly, as they are relevant to discovering what discipleship is and what it should do for us.

GENERAL CHARACTERISTICS OF DISCIPLESHIP

As a result of Jesus' sacrifice, as believers we have the Spirit of God permanently within us (Ephesians 1:13-14). The Father gave us His Spirit (John 14:26). He is to teach us (John 14:26). The Spirit speaks to us about what He hears in our hearts (John 16:12-16). The Spirit, as Teacher and Guide, speaks to our hearts about the specific application of God's Truth to our unique lives. This is the same Spirit who Authored the Scriptures, God's written Word (2 Timothy 3:16-17).

Discipleship involves learning from the Spirit, Who is available as part of our personal relationship with God. The beginning of discipleship, opening our hearts, involves learning *the elementary teachings of Christ*. The elementary teachings provide a foundation for mentally understanding the nature of our relationship with God, and generally the kinds of experiences we can expect to have as a result of that relationship. This part of discipleship, the elementary teachings, can be taught and learned in a classroom or lecture environment. As we understand those elementary teachings more and more, many real-life applications will become clear, and we begin to open our hearts to the changes in our lives which the Lord desires. However, this beginning part of discipleship is not the sum total of discipleship.

The totality of being discipled doesn't just involve learning that the Spirit plays a vital role in discipleship. It involves learning to interact with Him in our own life experiences. We can slip into thinking that the Spirit's primary method of teaching us is by reminding us about things we have learned from believers and God's written Word. We can call that discipleship, but all too often we run into application issues when such is the extent of our concept of discipleship. When our concept of discipleship focuses on knowledge versus how to open our hearts, we end up having the questions like the ones in the first two paragraphs of this chapter.

Discipleship isn't just concerned with learning information about the Scriptures, God and Satan, etc. **Learning the elementary teachings is to prepare us to move forward in discipleship, in order to learn where and how to interact more consistently with The Teacher, the Spirit of God.** This part of discipleship, which takes us beyond the elementary teachings of Christ, focuses heavily on the application of God's Divine Truth to our lives (Hebrews 6:1-3). This part of discipleship involves developing a critical skill: learning by the Spirit how to be taught continually by the Spirit in our hearts (1 John 2:27).

Discipleship involves learning *how* to learn from the Spirit when He speaks to us in our hearts. Discipleship is to teach us how to become *skillful* in experiencing God in our normal life circumstances. This involves application skills. Those skills are critical because while the Spirit can use anything and anyone to *try* to get us to hear what He seeks to teach us, whether we actually hear Him depends on what *we* do with the dynamics in our hearts and minds (1 John 3:18-24; 1 Thessalonians 5:19).

The skill of hearing The Teacher may be learned in a relatively short period of time if one is in a solid discipleship environment that goes beyond the elementary teachings of Christ. Still, we never outgrow the need to be discipled by the Spirit (John 14:26; 1 John 2:27). Much, if not most, of the Spirit's guidance to us is quite specific and deals with how we are to handle various life situations. His guidance isn't always given in advance. He usually gives His counsel on an "as the situation arises" basis.

Because we need the counsel of the Spirit to live for the Lord *throughout* life, being conformed to the image of the Lord is a lifelong effort. Being conformed to His image becomes more realistic when we can consistently hear and follow the guidance, teaching, and counsel of the Spirit whenever He is speaking. Being conformed to the Lord's image is a cooperative effort; we must do our part in learning to hear and submit to His Spirit (1 Thessalonians 5:19).

The Spirit tries not only to remind us daily of Scriptural teachings, He tries to tell us specifically how to live them in a given situation. We can discover when the Spirit is seeking to do this in us by learning how to pay attention to what is happening in our hearts (1 John 3:18-24). This is possible because God designed our hearts and minds to interact in ways that enable us to hear His voice. This means that when we recognize God's design, we can begin to recognize how to interact with fellow believers in order to improve our spiritual listening skills.

There have been many times when people (in the name of God and under the auspices of discipleship) have twisted and distorted God's Truth and cultivated relationships that do not reflect love and peace. It is important to be able to recognize the characteristics of relationships among believers that facilitate discipleship and being discipled. Those relationships are to help us be discipled and learn how to hear the voice of God for ourselves. While other believers may help us, the point of having the Spirit within you is to become skillful in hearing Him. This skill is vital to living well as a disciple of Christ.

Special Consideration:

When we use the term "disciple of Christ" or "disciples of Christ", we are not referring to a particular denomination or faith group. We are simply referring to believers, Christians in general. Christians were originally known as "disciples of Christ" (Acts 11:26). In using this terminology, we remind ourselves that as Christians, we are to be discipled and are to live as disciples. We will examine what that means exactly as we go along.

In addition to an ability to examine the Scriptures and speak to the Lord in prayer, being discipled involves examining how we live certain aspects of our daily lives. Skillful examination of our lives helps us to discover when we had opportunities to hear the Spirit and to recognize how well we actually heard Him. Our lives contain many application lessons that we must draw on. When we do draw on them, they help us learn how to cultivate a *two-way* interaction with God in much the same way we can have a dialogue with a wise friend.

It is profitable to study God's written Word in order to determine whether what we think God is saying to us is correct (2 Timothy 3:16-17). This is important due to Satan's presence, influence, and attacks. Satan's goals include influencing our ability to apply God's written Word to our lives. This means that the situations where Satan attacks us become the opportunities we may use to learn from and grow in the Spirit.

The real-life situations where Satan seeks to influence us are the situations we can use to be discipled. Many of our real-life situations and "normal" stresses and struggles are vast spiritual opportunities. The support and encouragement we can receive from fellow believers in spiritually intimate, personal relationships are vital to assisting us in learning to see Satan's attacks on us more clearly. Properly used in conjunction with Scriptural training, those relationships can help us hold ourselves accountable for whatever the Spirit tells us to do or not do when we are attacked and influenced by Satan.

Believers involved together in discipleship are not to seek to control one another. The concept of "you being held

A Disciple's Heart

accountable" means that you are responsible for examining your life when the Lord is speaking to you. Believers can help us with this when we commit ourselves to openly sharing when and where the Spirit is speaking to us. Believers can help us double-check our listening processes in very helpful ways once we understand the principles governing how to hear the Spirit of God. Still, it is inappropriate for one believer to try to force another believer to do or change something.

Counting the cost of living for God has always been requisite to following Jesus (Luke 14:26-35). Satan functions to make those costs seem unacceptable. Discipleship involves learning to listen to God for oneself and hearing Him speak to us individually about our specific costs. In being discipled in the company of other believers we may gain an increased awareness of the costs we might have to pay as individuals, but that is not inherently bad. Fellow believers may speak together about costs, but it is inappropriate for fellow believers to try to force them upon one another.

Being a disciple of Christ is not about being removed from the world altogether. When being discipled, some believers may find that the Spirit directs them to work for God in ways that others may consider to be more removed from the world. God's call to each of us is unique. But because being discipled focuses on applying God's Truth to our lives, when we are discipled, each of us may come to live quite differently from the world in a variety of ways. This is supposed to be characteristic of all believers. However, some believers handle living differently from the world more easily than others.

Living for the Lord includes learning to discover the Lord's will concerning areas of life where the Scriptures are silent. The Spirit of God speaks to a disciple of Christ about areas of life where the Scriptures may be silent. This is another reason why we never outgrow our need for the Spirit's counsel. To facilitate being discipled, believers can come together to focus on learning, individually, to hear the Spirit's guidance and counsel concerning life issues in which the written Word is silent.

Listening to the Spirit is NOT the same as speaking in tongues. Speaking in tongues is a different kind of interaction with the Spirit and is not the focus of this book. Listening to and hearing the Spirit in the way we are discussing is part of the daily interaction believers can cultivate in order to receive guidance, help, and answers from the Spirit who is providing them.

Finally, discipleship involves deliberate interactions to which a believer must intentionally choose to commit. Discipleship beyond the elementary teachings of Christ cannot be forced on a believer, nor can it be taught through lectures to a believer who is not ready to commit to being discipled beyond the elementary teachings of Christ. Discipleship beyond the elementary teachings is not something that happens *to* us, nor is it something that we can *do* to someone else. Discipleship beyond elementary teachings involves a kind of relationship in which a believer seeks *to be* discipled personally, openly and interactively.

What Does It Mean To "Go Beyond the Elementary Teachings of Christ?"

KEY CONCEPT:

Spiritual maturity does not come mainly by knowledge of the elementary teachings of Christ. Spiritual maturity comes by learning how to persevere and have faith, especially in uncomfortable and painful situations when some of those elementary teachings must be applied and capitalized upon. The Spirit seeks to teach and counsel us in that application; we must be trained.

Hebrews 6:1-3: "Therefore leaving the elementary teaching about the Christ, let us press on to maturity, not laying again a foundation of repentance from dead works and of faith toward God, of instruction about washings and laying on of hands, and the resurrection of the dead and eternal judgment. And this we will do, if God permits."

Hebrews 10:15-17: "And the Holy Spirit also testifies to us; for after saying, 'THIS IS THE COVENANT THAT I WILL MAKE WITH THEM AFTER THOSE DAYS, SAYS THE LORD: I WILL PUT MY LAWS UPON THEIR HEART, AND ON THEIR MIND I WILL WRITE THEM,' *He then says,* 'AND THEIR SINS AND THEIR LAWLESS DEEDS I WILL REMEMBER NO MORE.'" (Caps and italics are part of the translation.)

Hebrews 12:11: "All discipline for the moment seems not to be joyful, but sorrowful; yet to those who have been trained by it, afterwards it yields the peaceful fruit of righteousness."

Going beyond the elementary teachings of Christ involves learning to observe the dynamics in our hearts and minds. When we learn the elementary teachings of Christ (Hebrews 6:1-3) and our hearts begin to change in response, this is the work of the Spirit within us. It isn't just the words of the Scripture which changes our hearts. If it were simply the words that precipitated change, then everyone that read or heard them would change. When our hearts change, we are *participating* with the Spirit in ways that allow our hearts to change. There are certain dynamics that we are capitalizing on when our hearts change. There are also other dynamics we are capitalizing on when our hearts do not change.

When we are in some life situation and our hearts are disturbed, 1 John 3:18-24 tells us it is in that moment that the Spirit is speaking to us in our hearts. Hebrews 10:15-16 tells us why it is that with the heart we can be assured whether or not we understand the will of the Lord for us in a trying situation. Hebrews 12:11 discusses sorrow and situations that are not joyful — painful emotions are the kinds of emotions we often experience in trials.

Going beyond the elementary teachings involves learning from our trials. Trials are associated with the Lord's discipline. Hebrews 12:11 tells us we must be trained when the Lord is disciplining us through trials. We can say we are trained through a trial when our emotional experience in that particular trial shifts from sorrow or pain to become peaceful (Romans 5:3-5). The Spirit seeks to assist us in transformation by training us during our attempts to interact with Him, but He doesn't force us to be transformed during the trial (1 John 3:18-24).

Being discipled beyond the elementary teachings of Christ is what enables us to draw on the Spirit and learn to avoid sin. When we are not trained by the Lord's discipline during a trial and fail to accept or even recognize the lesson in the Lord's discipline, we sin. Hebrews 10:19 through Hebrews 12 discuss how sin is the result of lack of perseverance and faith when we know what God wants us to do, but the outcome of doing what He wants us to do is *uncertain* in terms of how the world might respond to us. Skillful interaction with the Spirit is essential to always being able to know what God wants us to do in a tough situation. Hebrews 11 provides examples of godly men and women who knew what God wanted them to do. They are examples of how God often asks godly people to act in order to fulfill His will and His Spirit's counsel.

Going beyond the elementary teachings of Christ involves recognizing when the Spirit is speaking. When the Spirit is speaking to us in real-life situations, hearing and understanding His counsel is what is to drive our actions as believers. The Spirit seeks to guide us into God's Truth about the lesson within the Lord's discipline, which is to influence how we respond to the real-life situations we face. Failure to hear the Spirit correctly often results in sin because we often respond to challenging situations according to our old patterns. Sometimes we sin because it is often hard to understand the "why" behind the Lord's discipline. When very difficult events happen to us, we wonder why the Lord would allow such things to happen *because* we are missing the lesson He seeks to give us.

When we say, "The Lord is disciplining me in such-and-such situation," we often draw very general conclusions as to the purpose of His lesson. We might think it is about faith, or maybe about being more loving, or about being more understanding or accepting of what we cannot control. These kinds of conclusions are often true, but in the course of being discipled beyond the elementary teachings, a believer consistently learns that the lesson in the Lord's discipline, and His guidance, is much more specific and personal in nature.

Going beyond the elementary teachings of Christ teaches us to hear the Spirit's counsel with clarity and in detail. When we are being disciplined, the Spirit is actually trying to tell us specifically what to say, do, ask, clarify, etc. When we correctly hear Him tell us those specific things to say, do, etc., those specifics may often *appear* to be self-defeating and self-destructive. According to the world, doing some of the things God tells us may actually be self-defeating. This does NOT mean God wants us to be doormats, nor does it mean that when multiple courses of action are open to us that God wants us to take the self-destructive course. It means we usually won't even consider courses of action that do not please us in some way unless we are picking the best of several distasteful courses of action. The only thing that makes the difference in knowing what is God's true will in such cases is the ability to actually hear the voice of the Lord with your heart clearly and consistently!

The Purpose of Discipleship

Take, for example, Abraham and God's directive for him to sacrifice Isaac (Genesis 22:1-10). The Lord stayed his hand, but Abraham didn't know that He would. Abraham had to know for sure what the Lord wanted of him, and Abraham had to be prepared to follow all the way through! We must be able to know what the Lord wants from us with as much certainty.

We usually dismiss Abraham's situation as different from ours because we believe the Lord communicated with Abraham audibly. Maybe the Lord did speak audibly, but if you will notice, whenever someone in the Bible says that the Lord said "...to me," the verb used is "said." To say means *not just* to say something "verbally," but "to communicate." This is true whether it is "the Lord said," or "Jesus said," or "John said," or "Moses said," or "the Spirit said" (Hebrews 3:7-11 is an example indicating the Spirit said some things to and through David).

Going beyond the elementary teachings of Christ means not just skillfully hearing the Spirit during trials, but skillfully working with him to transform the pain in our hearts. When we talk about transforming pain associated with the Lord's discipline so that we may experience peace, of what kinds of pain are we speaking? Psalm 38 describes the link between our heart disturbances, sin, and physical pains. Hebrews 12:11 indicates emotional pains are also experienced. The following are some examples of the kinds of emotional pain you may feel and be challenged to work with the Spirit to transform.

Anguish, weary, troubled, heavy-laden, grieved, distressed, mocked, anxiety, frustrated, fear, dread, anger, hopeless, lost or adrift, useless, overwhelmed, worn-out (emotionally), disgust, stressed, tense, annoyed, sad, depressed, bored, anxious, worried, concerned, rage, frightened, upset, aloof, dispassionate, disconnected, puzzled, inadequate, unloved, worthless, hateful, shame, guilt, melancholy, regretful, disappointed, envy, jealous, vengeful, empty, victimized, unappreciated, left out, abandoned, spurned powerless, lack, discouraged, scared, despair, uneasy, etc.

These kinds of emotional responses are disturbances in the heart; they disturb our peace. They often accompany trials and the Lord's discipline. While they are useful in that they indicate there is a spiritual issue the Spirit is speaking to, when such pains last for long periods of time, they can lead to various kinds of health problems. When emotional experiences are prolonged, it indicates we may profit from developing transformation skills. Hearing the Spirit well is directly related to our ability to transform those various forms of pain, and to our ability to properly persevere (Hebrews 10:19-39). The Spirit does not intend for those kinds of emotional experiences to go on and on; however, we must do our part in interacting with Him to transform those pains to peace (Romans 5:3-5).

Special Consideration:

From this point forward, when we talk about "transforming pain to peace," the above emotional responses are among the pains we must be able and prepared to transform. They indicate trials, and that spiritual issues are at stake. When we talk about hearing the Spirit speak to us in "painful or challenging situations," we are talking about the kinds of life situations where we might feel any of the above feelings. The above experiences are ones that disturb the peace we have in our hearts. They are "disturbances in the heart" and indicate times when we are experiencing the voice of the Spirit seeking to counsel, guide, and teach us. Throughout the reading, you may insert any of those emotional responses when you read the phrases "pain," "challenging situations," or "disturbances in the heart."

When peace seems to come over us easily during a trying situation, we are often unconsciously interacting with the Spirit through our hearts. We simply are not consciously paying attention to what is happening in our hearts. Going beyond the elementary teachings of Christ is to help us become consciously aware of what happens in our hearts when it changes easily, and when it is not changing as easily. This way, when the transformation task does not seem to happen quite as effortlessly, we can intentionally focus on those heart dynamics and participate with the Spirit, allowing Him to teach us and transform our hearts.

When our hearts are disturbed from a place of peace, that disturbance is the indicator that the Spirit is seeking to teach us *what* we need in that moment. The Spirit speaks and seeks to teach us something because we need His teaching, instruction, and counsel in order to live for the Lord in that moment. While we may accurately know Scriptural facts relevant to our situation, the Spirit's teaching often pertains to *how* to transform the heart and apply that knowledge. Interacting skillfully with the Spirit when we are being disciplined is what discipleship beyond the elementary teachings of Christ is all about.

The elementary teachings of Christ are critical. Without the elementary teachings, the goal of consistently interacting with the Spirit when He is speaking is not normally achievable. The elementary teachings are, therefore, part of discipleship because **they lay the foundation for us to *begin* learning *how* to be discipled by the Spirit when Satan attacks us in normal life situations.**

A Disciple's Heart

Today, the elementary teachings are typically presented in a classroom or lecture environment, i.e. Bible studies, special training classes, Sunday School and sermons. We teach and reiterate these important foundational concepts through various activities and programs. Elementary teachings concerning our relationship with Christ are important because many of them serve the specific purpose of pointing to the possibility of change, even from situations in everyday life when we are not in church. They show us what we are to experience in our interactions with Christ and the Spirit, Whom the Father gave us.

The nature of the elementary teachings of Christ is such that many applications to daily life become readily apparent. However, the elementary teachings are heavy on the informational side. Discussions about the elementary teachings may include discussing how to apply the teachings. But classes with larger audiences and the lecture-style presentations, in which elementary teachings may be taught, are usually not the most beneficial approaches to enable skillful examination of our own specific applications of the teachings.

Going beyond the elementary teachings of Christ focuses specifically on the personal application of Scriptural concepts to our everyday lives and circumstances, as this is what the Spirit often speaks to. As we mentioned, going beyond the elementary teachings involves *how* to discover *when* the Lord is challenging the disciple to persevere in faith in order to walk with God in daily situations (Hebrews 10:19 through Hebrews 12). This means that examining our own daily issues and challenges includes the "personal and private" issues we often do not discuss in church-classroom-like settings.

It is in our own matters of family, priorities, wants, past pains and wounds, etc., where we often find our trials and lingering issues pertaining to our hearts. In discipleship environments that focus specifically on going beyond the elementary teachings of Christ, the Scriptures are examined so we may observe some of the heart dynamics at work in people whose stories were recorded. This is the *part* of being discipled which helps us to understand why and how our heart dynamics are linked to the results that follow. But the discipleship environment is not a Bible study. When we study the Scriptures as part of going beyond the elementary teachings of Christ, the point is to learn how to hear the Spirit speaking to us and how to transform the pains and discomforts we often experience when we are disciplined and experience trials.

In many of our personal and private issues, we often simply try to "keep on keeping on." Going beyond the elementary teachings of Christ is to help us understand why perseverance is NOT about plowing through tough times or simply "forging ahead" when a painful situation cannot be changed. Perseverance is NOT about tolerating an uncomfortable situation until the first viable option for relief presents itself. Perseverance is NOT always about addressing an uncomfortable situation. Perseverance is about fighting the old self within you and changing to the new self. Perseverance involves trying to fight that fight consistently, at the Spirit's beckoning, and with His specific guidance on how to act externally and fight the old self/Satan internally.

Perseverance is required in order to keep up with the Spirit's teaching because His counsel and guidance corresponds to everyday life events (Galatians 5:16-26). **Perseverance is necessary in order to determine, in the moment He speaks, whether the Spirit is actually telling you to tolerate an uncomfortable situation, to address an uncomfortable situation, or to follow through with something else He already told you to do!** And while perseverance may involve dealing with a difficult situation *outside* of you, the true challenge of perseverance is dealing with the spiritual conflict some life situation precipitates *within* you. Consistency in transforming pain to peace is a "must-have" skill.

Going beyond the elementary teachings of Christ teaches us that there is a difference between *you making your own decision* on whether to accept or address something *while believing you are doing God's will*, versus actually involving the Spirit of God in your decision-making processes so that you do God's will. In a given moment when Satan attacks, you must *start* to do God's will by actually changing what the Spirit indicates you must change in you. This must be done *before* you can know whether the Spirit wants you to accept or address some aspect of the life situation you are facing! Read the last two sentences again! Having allowed the Lord to address changes in *you*, perseverance involves following through in demonstrating the changes the Lord has directed in you. This has to do with following through with whatever course(s) of action the Spirit directs you to take in terms of the external situation.

At first, hearing the Spirit of God can be uncomfortable as well as unfamiliar in its application to real-world, external situations. When you have an issue you are dealing with in life, say in regards to being able to provide for your family, you may experience some kind of inner conflict. You have questions. Do you get a new job? Do you stay with the old job? You know there is work to be done, research in the evening hours, not to mention all the other routine things which must be done in day-to-day living. Such times make it tough to be discipled beyond the elementary teachings of Christ, especially if other issues are confronting you at the same time.

When you are trying to be discipled beyond the elementary teachings of Christ during hectic times, you are facing a task that is not uncommon! You are seeking to identify and accept the Spirit's counsel of change in you. You are also seeking to transform inner pains into love and peace. And, in addition to that, you must also deal with the normal affairs of life!

When life gets busy and we face uncomfortable situations, we sometimes don't see the value of learning more about the elementary teachings of Christ, let alone going beyond those teachings. When life gets chaotic, time is at a premium, and we often conclude we do not have enough of it to participate in the "extras." We don't have time for extra teachings that don't bear directly on the decision-making challenges we face in the critical moment. These times are, however, among the times when discipleship beyond the elementary teachings is most relevant and practical. During such times we have the kinds of experiences that are very useful opportunities to be discipled beyond the elementary teachings. The Spirit has much to say during these times. The emotional and emotive dynamics in our hearts indicate that this is true.

Learning to hear and obey the Spirit's voice can be a struggle when the train of life is up to full speed, and then we realize the Lord is trying to make some corrections within us. Part of the cost of serving Him is persevering in hearing His voice when it is tough! This affects us greatly! The challenges that come with simply creating time to learn how to connect with Him can seem to enflame the inner conflict that we fundamentally want to go away. In this way, following Christ involves taking on a cross which unbelievers avoid by simply making their decisions and fulfilling their desires. This cross may appear heavy, but only when we aren't skilled in understanding how we are being asked to surrender to the Lord (Matthew 11:28-29). When we drag out our learning processes by plowing through the busy times in life, we are in effect often resisting the voice of the Spirit. As a result, the burden feels heavy because of ourselves, not because of God.

In Hebrews 6, the writer says the recipients need to grow up spiritually. From Hebrews 6:13 to 10:18, the writer provides extensive supporting material leading up to a discussion on the practical application of perseverance — that which is beyond the elementary teachings of Christ (Hebrews 10:19-39). Hebrews 11 then provides numerous examples where faith was demonstrated in situations where, *if they were happening to us, we would typically believe God would not ask us to make such sacrifices.* This is the point! How will we know the Spirit's specific direction, overcome doubt, and have faith if we cannot hear Him well or consistently because we are too busy? How will we know what God wants today when we forget what His Spirit counseled us on yesterday? Perseverance and faith are especially critical when we are being discipled beyond the elementary teachings of Christ because going beyond those teachings is often best learned when life is racing by!

Because hearing the voice of God is a spiritual skill at the most foundational and essential level, spiritual maturity is not measured in years but hinges on *learning* one thing well:

> *How to allow the Lord to specifically and continually direct our actions, lifestyles, attitudes, preferences, desires, opinions, etc., by learning to listen to Him giving that specific direction through His Spirit in our hearts, especially when life situations are accompanied by emotions within us.*

Discipleship beyond the elementary teachings of Christ requires us to use our God-permitted life experiences to learn how to do that one thing. Once it is grasped, a disciple can consistently learn directly from the Spirit of God without a human teacher (1 John 2:27). This does not mean we ever outgrow our need of the Body of Christ. It does mean that continual change is only possible in Christ one uncomfortable situation at a time because it is then that the Spirit of God is frequently speaking to that change.

Special Consideration 1:

From this point forward, when we use the terms "discipleship" or "being discipled," we are specifically referring to the aspect of discipleship that goes beyond the elementary teachings of Christ. We are referring to cultivating our ability in Christ to apply God's divine Word to our lives by interacting skillfully with the Spirit. We are referring to our potential, as believers in Christ, to do our part by developing the skill of hearing the voice of the Spirit with our hearts, the skill of transforming emotional pain to peace, and the skill of submitting our hearts to Christ so that we might realize the new self He seeks to cultivate within us during a specific real-life, uncomfortable situation.

Special Consideration 2:

Also, from this point forward, when we use the term "human teacher", we are specifically referring to a human teacher that is among those described by 1 John 2:27. This kind of human teacher is capable of discipling believers to go beyond the elementary teachings of Christ. This kind of human teacher is capable of teaching believers the "how to" of interacting with and experiencing the Spirit of God in the way the Scriptures often demonstrate. This kind of human teacher may serve in a variety of roles within the Body of Christ. However, a believer's ability to teach a Sunday School class or a Bible study, or a believer's position as a deacon, lay leader, or other leader within the body do not necessarily indicate they are, or are called to be, human teachers who disciple believers beyond the elementary teachings of Christ. Some believers in these positions are called to serve as human teachers *of* the elementary teachings, not as human teachers that disciple *beyond* the elementary teachings. This is mentioned now because we will be examining *what* this kind of human teacher teaches and the kinds of environments in which this aspect of discipleship is taught. What this book, and 1 John 2:27, means by a human teacher is somewhat different from what we experience with some human teachers today.

DISCIPLESHIP ENVIRONMENTS AND THE NEED THEY FULFILL

KEY CONCEPT:

Generally speaking, a believer can be discipled beyond the elementary teachings of Christ in three environments. Each environment is different based on the personal relationships the believer needs to have with other believers in order to interact, or learn to interact, consistently with the Spirit. The purpose of those relationships with other believers is to teach a believer to examine his own life and learn how to apply God's Truth to it by hearing the Spirit of God within the heart.

1. Being discipled one-on-one by the Spirit of God without need for a human teacher (1 John 2:27). For this to be the primary means of discipleship beyond the elementary teachings of Christ, *skill* in hearing the Spirit is required. To acquire that skill and consistency usually requires preparation and discipling from one of the other two discipleship environments.

2. Being discipled by the Spirit through the use of a human teacher. This may occur both one-on-one and/or in a group of disciples. There are many examples in the Scriptures, and include Paul, Stephen, Timothy, Phillip, etc.

3. Being discipled by the Spirit, without a human teacher, through the use of a group of believers in a fellowship that facilitates discipleship beyond the elementary teachings of Christ. The letters to the Corinthians and Galatians demonstrate that when their human teachers departed, fellowship for discipleship was the environment they were in.

The three discipleship environments are modeled by the examples of Jesus, His disciples, and New Testament believers. Some specifics about discipleship are given in the Scriptures, but on the whole the Scriptures reveal more of how it was demonstrated. While the Key Concept (above) specifies the three discipleship environments, the Scriptures often did not present them distinctly because they were being demonstrated in real life, and even in the writing of the letters of the New Testament.

That there are three discipleship environments does *not* mean they are *always* distinct, stand-alone environments even though they may be. The New Testament reveals that some believers were clearly in one particular discipleship environment for extended periods of time. In many cases this is because the human teachers traveled quite a bit. Generally speaking, most believers began the process of being discipled beyond the elementary teachings of Christ either in fellowship or with a human teacher (Paul is an example of an exception).

The letters to the Corinthians, the Galatians, and Hebrews are three examples of how the discipleship environments were not always stand-alone environments. When human teachers like Paul, Stephen, Timothy, etc. were present among believers, the believers with them were experiencing the human teacher discipleship environment. When the human teachers moved on to another town, they left some believers capable of relating the elementary teachings of Christ. Those who were selected or approved to teach the elementary teachings were not necessarily human teachers who discipled others beyond the elementary teachings of Christ. It takes time, real-life experiences, and an ability to interact with the Spirit in order for the Spirit to grow human teachers. While some believers in Corinth, for example, may have been able to be discipled one-on-one by the Spirit, this did not necessarily make them human teachers.

1 Corinthians indicates the believers in Corinth were frequently in the fellowship for discipleship environment. In other words, they often had no human teacher present and were supposed to be interacting in fellowship to learn to interact with and grow in the Spirit. 1 Corinthians 2 indicates the Corinthians were not being discipled by the Spirit one-on-one, nor were they learning to be discipled by the Spirit from their fellowships.

In Corinth, different believers had experienced different human teachers: Apollos, Paul, Cephas. While the human teachers had laid the foundation in the elementary teachings of Christ, that foundation did not represent the sum total of growth in Christ (1 Corinthians 3:1-2). The human teachers sought to enable various groups of Corinthians to fellowship for discipleship (1 Corinthians 3:6); still, the fellowship for discipleship environments fell apart. The believers began to quarrel among themselves based on who their human teachers had been. The believers fell into division after their human teachers moved on (1 Corinthians 1:11-12). This led to all sorts of problems in terms of the basics of interacting with one another as one body, and also with their ability to live according to the elementary teachings themselves. Paul speaks to some of those problems throughout his first letter to the Corinthians.

The Purpose of Discipleship

Paul said the believers in Corinth were worldly and were spiritual infants (1 Corinthians 3:1-2). He also said he was thankful he only baptized a handful of believers (1 Corinthians 1:14-15). These are not the characteristics of a body of believers being discipled by effective human teachers capable of demonstrating how to hear the voice of God within. In other words, that the spiritual needs of the Corinthians were not being met indicates the discipleship approach for the Corinthians was not that of a human teacher environment but of fellowship for discipleship.

In light of the Corinthians' problems, Paul hoped Timothy would go to visit them (1 Corinthians 16:10). This is an example of how a New Testament human teacher would often return to assist believers who had not yet developed the various skill sets that knowledge of the Scriptures indicates is possible. The letter to the Corinthians demonstrates that the human teacher often laid the foundation for fellowship for discipleship. It demonstrates that the only thing that would enable fellowship for discipleship to produce spiritual growth was the ability to interact with the Spirit. In 2 Corinthians 2:6-16, Paul describes why the ability to interact with the Spirit, which is the goal of fellowship for discipleship, is so necessary and critical.

In seeking any discipleship environment there are certain risks, as well as benefits, which we must consider.

A Disciple's Heart

Discipleship Environment	Benefit	Risk
Disciple of Christ consistently able to hear the voice of the Spirit of God; no need of a human teacher.*	Without another person's assistance: consistently able to deliberately and clearly identify Satan's attack, discover Satan's deception in own heart, able to hear the Spirit's guidance on changes God's will requires for himself, and able to consistently and deliberately discover God's will as told by the Spirit.	Incorrectly estimating one's ability to do these things is serious old self deception. Person is not only Satan's tool without knowing it, but is a spiritual danger to others who may seek guidance from this person.
Disciple of Christ being discipled by a human teacher to learn to hear the voice of the Spirit of God.**	You are able to receive guidance from a person who can do the above for himself and is able to teach you how to listen to the Spirit for yourself. Able to see that the human teacher will not get in the Spirit's way even if you inadvertently ask, "What should I do?" or say, "Tell me what to do." You are responsible to live your life.	If you incorrectly hear the Spirit and make a poor choice in a human teacher, you will be led astray and it may take you a while to figure that out.
Disciple of Christ fellowshipping with believers to learn how to hear the voice of the Spirit of God.***	When a human teacher is not available, you can fellowship with other believers to focus on learning the things listed in the top block of this column.	You are in a group with people who also aren't trained in listening to God. Can rapidly become "blind leading the blind." Very easy to vent instead of learning to hear the Spirit. Easy to avoid discussing application and not learn transformation. Easy to think knowledge equals correct living.

* In order for most of us to get to this discipleship environment where we have no need for a human teacher's assistance, we usually require training which comes from one or both of the other two discipleship environments.

** It is very possible to teach and preach the gospel message, using the Scriptures, without being skilled in hearing God's Spirit consistently. When we do teach and preach the gospel without that skill, we are pointing the way to becoming a disciple of Christ while we still have our own need to learn to interact with the Spirit. The Scriptures indicate that this often happened, and it isn't necessarily a problem, but it could be.

*** Fellowship for discipleship requires that the participants are somewhat familiar with the fundamental Scriptural principles of listening to God, as well as the heart dynamics which make that possible. A fellowship in which believers aren't familiar with those things will find that Luke 6:37-42 applies.

Regardless which of the three discipleship environments we may seek out, all three are supposed to help us in certain common ways to go beyond the elementary teachings of Christ. **All three discipleship environments are to help us learn how to live for God and apply God's Truth to our lives. All three discipleship environments help us learn to live in godly ways given the following spiritual attributes of the current human condition.**

1. Satan has the ability *to attempt* to deceive mankind. This has been "permitted" or "allowed" by God since the Garden of Eden.

2. The Spirit has the ability *to attempt* to communicate to us in our hearts about Satan's deceptions, about the changes we must make as individuals, and about God's plan of action for us individually in each situation where Satan attacks us. But we can quench the Spirit (1 Thessalonians 5:19).

3. God's design of our hearts and minds permit us:

    a. To make spiritual choices (everyday choices that carry spiritual implications) based on limited and/or inaccurate spiritual information. We have the ability to be deceived, which includes the ability to distract ourselves, in sinful ways, from pain associated with the Lord's disciplines during the spiritual war.

    b. To become aware of the spiritual nature of spiritual choices. We can cultivate our ability to hear the Spirit speaking to us. This includes cultivating the ability to transform pain to peace consistently, without needing distractions, each time the Lord's discipline is unpleasant (Hebrews 12:11).

    c. To have free will, which includes the choice to increase

or decrease the abilities listed in *a* and *b* above.

4. Free will does NOT include the choice to participate in the spiritual war; everyone is in the spiritual war.

5. Free will comes with the requirement to make spiritual choices when they arise in real life situations, whether we recognize them or not. We do NOT get to choose *when* they arise. And when spiritual choices arise, we cannot avoid choosing between God and Satan.

6. Jesus' sacrifice did not change any the above five attributes.

7. Jesus' sacrifice did ensure that, as believers, we are *forgiven* when Satan succeeds in deceiving us and we fail to live as God would have us live. Jesus' sacrifice did provide the *permanent* indwelling of the Holy Spirit to help us succeed in living as God would have us to given the attributes above — i.e., to live for God.

Together, these spiritual attributes of the current human condition have great bearing on us as individuals, on the experiences we have, and on our understanding of how and why the spiritual war includes us in various "emotional" situations. They indicate our need to be led by the Spirit of the Lord in all situations when Satan is seeking to deceive us. They also indicate that Jesus' sacrifice demands our awareness of and active involvement in the spiritual dynamics within us when Satan is attacking us personally.

Together, these attributes imply the *outline* of the purpose of discipleship: to learn by the Spirit how to be taught by the Spirit. This is the same dynamic as when we let the Spirit convince us of our need to be saved. The discipleship environment in which Jesus left His disciples was with the ability to be taught by the Spirit directly and consistently without a human teacher. John

16:12-16 facilitated the accomplishment of Matthew 28:19-20. The *skill and consistency* that facilitates the one-on-one discipleship environment with the Spirit is NOT automatically embraced by a believer (Ephesians 3:16-19). That skill is like any other in that it must be cultivated and requires discipline to develop. Discipleship beyond the elementary teachings of Christ is to help develop that skill. We can see that interacting with the Spirit is possible to experience on a highly consistent basis, and the evidence is in our own lives. We have *all* heard the Spirit's voice correctly at one time or another, and it is the Lord's will that we do so regularly.

To assist believers in developing consistency in listening to the Spirit, one-on-one and consistently, we may either be discipled by a human teacher or in a fellowship of believers that focuses on discipleship. When a believer, as a result of his own personal assessment, becomes aware of the need to learn how to consistently hear the Spirit within, something happens: the believer is beginning to acknowledge that he is lacking in the ability to be discipled one-on-one by the Spirit. The other two environments of discipleship may then become helpful.

So, how are you meeting your discipleship needs? Are you confident in *your* ability to consistently hear the Spirit tell you all things you need to live out your daily life in the way God intends? Are you being discipled beyond the elementary teachings of Christ? Do you have a need to be discipled by either a human teacher or in fellowship with other believers? Do you have a solid understanding of the dynamics of the heart and of the principles of listening to the voice of God in your heart? Your answers to these questions are based on three things:

1. Whether or not you have developed the spiritual skill of listening to the Spirit of God speaking specifically to you through your heart during real-life situations.

2. Whether you believe your daily experience of God is lacking in any way and, if so, what you are willing to let His Spirit tell you to do about it without taking things in your own hands.

3. Whether or not you have developed the spiritual skill of transforming pain or discomfort associated with the Lord's discipline into peace without deviating from the Spirit's counsel.

ESSENTIALS FOR GOING BEYOND THE ELEMENTARY TEACHINGS OF CHRIST

If we examine ourselves and seek to be discipled beyond the elementary teachings of Christ, there is some foundational knowledge and awareness which is extremely useful in avoiding certain obstacles we are likely to encounter. The elementary teachings and instruction should provide the following as part of the beginning of discipleship.

KEY CONCEPT:

To be discipled beyond the elementary teachings of Christ in ANY of the three discipleship environments, a believer must have the following:

1. An awareness of his own *need* to learn how to *consistently* apply God's written Word and to hear the Spirit's spoken counsel in daily life (John 14:25-26, 16:12-14).

2. A basic understanding of and familiarity with the tools necessary to study the Scriptures, authored by the Spirit of God (2 Timothy 3:16-16).

3. A basic understanding of the dynamics of our hearts and

minds. In other words, God designed our hearts and minds to work and interact such that in any situation we may either come to know His will or be deceived (1 John 3:18-24).

4. A basic understanding of the Scriptural principles dealing with how to listen to the Spirit of God with the heart (1 Corinthians 2:10-13). This leads to the ability to be taught consistently by the Author of the Scriptures, Who permanently dwells within us (1 John 2:27).

5. Personal relationships that facilitate being discipled, which include practical examinations of our daily living application(s) in any one of the three discipleship environments (Romans 12:2; 2 Corinthians 13:5).

We have already been discussing the first essential in the Key Concept above: an awareness of one's own need to learn how to consistently apply God's written Word and to consistently hear His spoken counsel in daily life. In the next few pages we will examine each of the other essentials from the Key Concept above.

Let's examine the second essential from the Key Concept above: a basic understanding of and familiarity with the tools necessary to study the Scriptures. This skill is only essential *because* the Scriptures were authored by the Spirit of God! We are speaking of the same Spirit of God who speaks to you in your heart! We have already discussed this a little too, but it cannot be overemphasized. The same Author of the Scriptures is speaking to you in your heart about the issues, challenges, obstacles, traps, etc. that you encounter in your daily life! The same Holy Spirit, Who authored what is in Scripture, is seeking to converse with you concerning the daily, real life, and nuts and bolts application of what is in the written Word of God!

What is meant by "basic familiarity with the tools to study

Scripture"? It does not mean that discipleship beyond the elementary teachings is a Bible study. But a Bible study may help teach you how to use the Scriptures, which you will need as you learn how to apply God's Truth to your life by learning to listen to The Teacher — the Spirit speaking in your heart. You will need to study the dynamics in the lives of people in the Scriptures. This will help you to effectively examine your own painful life situations where you were not able to reference the written Word of God, but where you had full access to the Spirit within. The Scriptures demonstrate how the dynamics of the heart and mind can be properly used and applied to daily living. They demonstrate how others were often driven to act in certain ways during their real-life struggles, and whether the dynamics in their hearts were godly or not, and why.

To help you use the Bible to develop your interaction with the Spirit and live God's Truth, it is important to be able to discover the context of what is being said. Today there are many tools and books available to help you figure out the context of any given passage. You need to be able to find out basic things like what a Pharisee is; whether Paul knew the people to whom he wrote; what the recipients' culture was like, etc.

Scriptural roles and relationships are important to recognize and understand. God's guidance for us is based on the roles we are in and on the relationships we have with others. God's guidance to us does not remove us from the world or make us independent from the world. However, while God's guidance to us will sometimes require us to act independently, the roles and relationships between us and others are factors which both the Lord and Satan use to move us in certain directions. A key part of getting the context of something means we cannot disregard the *spiritual* basis for roles and relationships. It also means that when we alter roles and relationships from the way they appear in the Scriptures, we are also altering the application in some way. That

The Purpose of Discipleship

is important, need-to-know information.

Becoming familiar with the Scriptures means having a good Bible dictionary, and timelines can be very useful to recognize what was happening historically. It is helpful to have a mental picture of not only what was written but *when* it was written; that often relates to *why* it was written. For example, there is an order to *when* letters were written in the New Testament, but the letters are not presented in the order in which they were originally written. Paul's letters are presented where his longest letters are first and his shortest letters are last; they are not in chronological order in our Bibles.

A study Bible is helpful. It provides introductions to the individual books, helpful side notes and a basic concordance to assist in identifying similar and other relevant passages. A study Bible can help you discover that everything in the Scriptures was written to assist the recipients in understanding something, including you. This starts you in the direction of seeing relationships between life events, Satan's activities, and the Lord's activities. Recognizing those relationships is something you will need to do well to hear the Spirit speaking to you.

If, for example, in the course of your own learning to listen to God processes, you came to examine the long lineages recorded in the book of Numbers, you would need to know why those lineages were important to the people in the Scriptures. Then, you may want to consider your own family's history. There is a spiritual relevance to the lines of our families. The lineages in the Scriptures influenced the lives of the descendants; how has your family's history influenced yours? The history in the Scriptures often provides a basis for an identity for those who follow; how has our culture, history and identity influenced your own identity, your values, and your life? Sometimes these questions are very germane. These kinds of questions help you to begin to recognize the dynamics in the hearts of others so you may begin to see them in yourself, even though your life situations may be different from theirs.

A study Bible can help in other ways. If you want to discover how New Testament believers were taught to love one another, you would develop a distorted view of love if you seek to do a Bible study on 1 Corinthians 13 alone. You must be able to examine the actions of believers across multiple books and letters to discover how believers interacted with one another in love. Again, the tools we are discussing will help you research examples of how believers interacted, in love, when a believer continually failed to turn from sinful ways, when a spouse made poor or ungodly decisions, or when life was not going the way believers might have liked it to go.

Often we fail to appreciate the Old Testament. Some believers think it was superseded by Jesus and so is not as relevant. There are relationships between the Old and New Testaments. Paul says that a study of the Scriptures is profitable (2 Timothy 3:16-17). That means that Paul is saying a study of the Old Testament (the only Scriptures he had), is profitable, even to us as Christians. We must discover why it is profitable now, even though Jesus has fulfilled the law, and even though many of us are not Jewish.

Part of being familiar with the Scriptures means you need to be able to think clearly when you study them. Don't gloss over a passage assuming that because you have read it a hundred times you have grasped everything. There are many good books which can help you with this task. Check yourself to be sure you approach each reading with fresh eyes; ask questions and look for your own assumptions, then check to see if your assumptions are valid in comparison to your own real-life experiences. This can help you ask skillful questions about your own application skills. Keep a list of issues and real-life questions you are unable to answer satisfactorily. Also, be aware that what you understand the Spirit to be telling *you* can be adversely influenced by others if you are not very careful. This is another reason why having the tools to study the Scriptures is important.

Because the Scriptures are to help you learn to listen to God and to learn how to live your daily life, **application is vital!** This does NOT mean you are always supposed to do what so-and-so in the Bible did. For example, just because the prophets did this or that doesn't mean you are supposed to do the same. This is especially true if you have recognized *your own need* to learn to listen to God's voice consistently with your heart and are seeking to be discipled by a human teacher or in a fellowship for discipleship.

Let's examine the third essential from the Key Concept above: a basic understanding of how God designed your heart and mind to work and interact. To acquire that, you will need to study God's written Word *and* you will need to study you! Being able to move beyond Scriptural knowledge to consistency in godly living requires understanding the dynamics of your heart and mind. It is really easy to dissect the written Word of God and have thoughts about times in your life when such things applied, but it is a completely different eye-opening experience to really identify the ways you often live according to Satan's influence!

Satan's undetected influences cause us to act in accordance with patterns. If you are seeking to live the way God would have you to live without living according to the patterns of the world (Romans 12:2), then you must not only be aware of the world's patterns (patterns influenced by Satan), but of how they manifest in your own life. Whether we follow those patterns or not is determined by how we use our hearts and minds. Usually we are not as consciously involved in using our hearts and minds as we believe we are.

When we study ourselves under Satan's influence, we are NOT just studying life *before* we chose to live for the Lord. No. We are NOT even *partially* off limits from Satan's attacks because we are believers. The concept is to get to know the vigor of our old selves, and in so doing we will *begin* to discover the times the Lord has been speaking to us yet we did not hear Him. Those are the times when Satan is successful. There is much that can be said about understanding how our hearts and minds work, but once we learn how to pay attention, the Scriptures can speak to us in ways we did not imagine possible. This helps greatly in real-life application and interacting with the Spirit.

When we understand the dynamics of the heart and mind, we begin to see many areas of our lives which need improvement. In other words, we become more aware of failures, not just from our past, but in our present. This can be quite discomforting. We do not usually enjoy feeling like we are failing the Lord. Awareness of our recent failures causes us to ask, "How do I change?" "What does the Lord want me to do to deal with these areas in which I am not living well for Him?" These kinds of questions require us to know some specifics about God's will for us. To get those specifics, we need to improve our ability to interact with the Lord and His Spirit when He is speaking to us.

Let's examine the fourth essential from the Key Concept above: a basic understanding of the Scriptural principles dealing with how to listen to the Spirit of God with your heart. It is important to be able to couple this essential skill with a familiarity of the tools used to study the Scriptures and a basic understanding of the dynamics of the heart and mind.

To understand why people in the Scriptures did what they did, then first the condition of that person's heart and mind must be coupled with some of your own training in and awareness of the heart and mind dynamics. That must be coupled with a basic understanding of the Scriptural principles which govern how we can listen to the voice of God. When heart dynamics are brought together with the principles behind hearing the voice of God, you will begin to discover a structure for being able, not only to hear the Spirit, but to understand what He is saying and why. Couple that with a solid study of the patterns of your old self and you will begin to see the spiritual war as it has, is and will likely continue unfolding in your life until you become more consistent in listening to the Spirit of God with your heart, and living according to His counsel.

By developing and linking these essential spiritual skills together, you will be able to see patterns in the Lord's counsel to your heart. You will see that those patterns correspond to patterns in the attacks Satan typically mounts against you in various situations. Identifying these patterns is crucial in discovering the real-life applications the Spirit speaks to you about. They help you recognize that Satan's attacks against you are sometimes different than from Satan's attacks on others. The differences are based not only on the condition of the hearts of others, but also on your own heart condition. Also, in learning to bring these skills together, you begin to see how your memories, thoughts, wants, desires, goals, etc. are all very important in the context of the moments that you have them.

Training in these concepts and skills is what makes our need to learn to hear God extremely apparent. **This is when the fifth essential from the Key Concept above becomes uncompromisingly vital to discipleship: personal relationships that facilitate discipleship.** Because the spiritual context and nature of our experiences are so relevant to real-life application, the support, encouragement, and sharing that can happen in discipleship environments with other believers creates very strong bonds between believers. Those bonds are critical and vital for overcoming the rocks and thorns in life (Matthew 13:14-23; Mark 4:10-20). Those bonds are bonds of spiritual intimacy which are not common in our country today. We will examine the nature of these personal relationships as we progress.

A Personal Relationship with God Involves Personal Interaction with His Spirit

It is possible at any time for a believer to begin learning to continually experience the two-way personal relationship with the Spirit in real time. This is because of the *permanent* indwelling of God's Spirit in believers. The Holy Spirit of God was given to us because of Jesus' sacrifice, and it demonstrates the lengths to which God has gone to communicate His desire for us to hear and know Him.

Prior to the day of Pentecost, the Spirit was less tolerant of those who claimed to live for the Father and failed. When God saw that the heart and life of a person did not sufficiently match the words and actions of the person, the Spirit often departed from that person altogether (Psalms 51:11; 1 Samuel 16:13-14; Isaiah 63:9-11).

Today, if we truly believe in the Son and at various times fail to live according to God's intent, the Spirit doesn't leave us. In a moment of sin, the Spirit is quenched and Satan is being successful. Yet we are often unaware when we are quenching the Spirit. Specifically, that statement means that often we are unaware not only of *how* Satan is attacking us personally but even *when* he is attacking. We are also frequently unaware of the full impact Satan's attacks have on our choices. This is because we often do not recognize the relationship between the emotional disturbances in our hearts, Satan's attacks, and the Spirit's voice.

The essence of going beyond the elementary teachings of Christ focuses on how the personal relationship with Jesus Christ includes a personal *interaction* with the Holy Spirit, who is also God, the Father's Spirit (Ephesians 4:30), and who is also the Spirit of Christ (Acts 16:6-7; Romans 8:9-11; 2 Corinthians 17; 1 Peter 1:10-12). If these concepts appear new to you, you may want to study the Spirit's presence and activities in the Old Testament, the several New Testament Scriptures which corroborate that, as well as studying the nature of the Trinity — one God, three persons. You also may want to review the significance of the permanent indwelling of the Spirit versus what the conditions are for, and the length of, a "non-permanent" indwelling of the Spirit. This is what often happened prior to Jesus' sacrifice.

A personal relationship with Jesus includes a personal interaction with Him which is of the Spirit. This interaction with the Spirit is NOT nebulous and is NOT something He does *to* you. Again, this interaction is NOT about "speaking in tongues," that is a different interaction by the Spirit described in the Scriptures. Hearing the Spirit speaking is a necessary, reoccurring interaction, and it specifically involves hearing His guidance, counsel, and teaching to you in your heart. This kind of listening is about *active* listening, not passive.

How can you know if you can hear the Spirit well? Ask yourself whether you consistently hear the Spirit speaking as clearly as you can read the words on this page, whenever you experience difficult or uncomfortable situations, whenever you struggle with making a decision, or whenever you recognize you aren't at peace. If you can't hear Him well or consistently in those kinds of situations, then you can improve your listening skills, and you have a need to be discipled. If you wonder what the Lord wants of you in a given situation, if it sometimes takes you a while to recognize what He wants you to do, or if you hear Him *sometimes*, then you have the need to be discipled beyond the elementary teachings of Christ, so you can improve your listening skills.

Remember, learning *how* to listen consistently is not supposed to be a skill that it takes a lifetime to develop. Exercising the skill of listening to the Spirit consistently and following through in faith with what He tells you is the lifetime effort. In other words, you are supposed to be certain about what God wants of you in a given challenging situation. Being able to know exactly what the Spirit is saying is a skill that all believers may develop. Following through consistently with the Spirit's counsel (God's will), once we know it, is the part that we must work on throughout our entire lives. Being discipled can help you learn to do your part of interacting with the Spirit better and make your relationship with God stronger and more practical than any other relationship you have.

While we may speak to God in prayer, read His written Word and experience His presence in other believers, a *two-way* interaction with the Lord happens through our hearts. Unfortunately, the dynamics of the heart which permit that interaction are not always well understood. We can see this for ourselves in our own lives. We can see it during experiences where our connection with the Lord is such that we do not have a sense of peace. When we lose our sense of inner peace, it often seems to happen because whatever is going on around us is somehow dampening our connection with God. We may be around other believers or we may be reading God's Word, but something about the heart has changed such that we aren't experiencing our true connection with Him. Perhaps we are not separated from God altogether, but whatever has happened within the heart has resulted in an experience where we certainly do not feel the calming, loving and peaceful connection we feel at other times.

The Purpose of Discipleship

It is important to make a distinction between reading God's written Word and listening to God's voice in your heart. Making the distinction is vital in order to recognize that we are interacting with God in our hearts in certain ways when we actually hear God while studying His written Word. When we don't hear God, something else is going on in our hearts. This doesn't happen because the Scriptures are useless, it is because the heart was not in tune. The heart is the key. The heart is the spiritual "earpiece" to which God speaks so that we will change the interaction between the heart and mind. Our ability to listen to what God is saying whenever He speaks to us, no matter where we are or what we are doing, hinges on the dynamics in the heart.

Whether we are studying the written Word or doing the normal, regular activities of life, Satan may come to work against us. When Satan attacks us, the Spirit speaks to our hearts to inform us about the attack, to remind us of who we are in Christ, to tell us what we must accept or change about ourselves in Christ, and to tell us how to act in response to that attack. The Spirit is trying to do a lot in and for us, but we must be able to hear Him skillfully to avoid quenching Him inadvertently. Part of what Satan seeks to do is cause us to fail to recognize the attack in the first place. When Satan is successful, we do not seek to hear the voice of God during the attack because we aren't recognizing our need in that moment. When we do recognize the attack, Satan seeks to distort, twist and convolute the voice of God in our hearts. When Satan is successful, we are enabling that success by quenching the Spirit's voice within us. Discipleship functions to help us become skilled in living for God by discovering, in our own daily and normal lives, how Satan works against us and how not to quench the Spirit.

When, in a given situation, Satan is nurturing a seed of sin in you, you need to hear the Spirit's instruction due to the deceptive nature of Satan's influence. An influence *is* deceptive when, to you, it appears to be one thing and, in fact, from God's view it is actually something else. That means that without hearing the Spirit's teaching in that moment, you will not see Satan's deception for what it is. The Spirit's instruction involves change because Satan's influence encourages your old self, and you must pass the old away in order to be in the new self.

When you really see your need and you want to hear the Spirit's counsel, you experience a sense of urgency in your life. When you are really willing to accept continual change, you long for God's help in "getting out of the box" which Satan continually works to build around you. If you have the courage and desire to discover how the Lord wants you to handle situations of all difficulty levels (great and seemingly insignificant), then you are prepared to be discipled in a way that comes with intention beyond classroom teaching, classroom interactions, and lectures.

This is not to say that until you sign up for a "discipleship class" you haven't been interacting with the Spirit. All believers have experienced the Spirit's teaching at certain points in their lives without realizing how to experience it on a continuing basis.

Based on your own experience of walking with God, you have probably realized by now that we usually don't get all the answers at once. Most often it is just one answer that applies to a particular situation. Many times we get stuck trying to figure out what the Lord wants us to do in a particular situation when our hearts are disturbed. Sometimes we interpret that to mean "wait." Being able to skillfully interact with the Spirit helps us to identify why we get stuck and how to get unstuck. Many times the "wait" answer may not actually be God's instruction to wait. Sometimes His answers appear that way because we aren't that skilled in the two-way relationship with the Spirit.

The Purpose of Discipleship

When we are longing for an answer or solution to a problem and aren't hearing from the Lord, we sometimes *assume* that the Spirit isn't speaking. We often choose to trust that His solution will come in time because we do not hear Him giving us a solution. When we *assume* He isn't speaking, even though we are longing for an answer or solution, we *assume* we can make choices and act by continuing to do whatever we are used to doing, or by making our own decisions according to our desires. These assumptions lead to sin.

We act as if it is the Spirit's job to "break through" to us, knowing that He could if He wanted to do so. While the Spirit does break through to us in some situations, it is important to realize that we are playing a part in permitting that breakthrough. We are not quenching the Spirit in that situation (1 Thessalonians 5:19)! When we overlook our responsibility as believers to fulfill our part of submitting to the Lord, or when we think we play a minor part in the Spirit being able to get through our old self thinking, then it becomes very easy to assume we can hear His Spirit's voice well most all of the time. This is potentially a spiritually dangerous assumption. We can and must cultivate our ability in Christ to fulfill our responsibility, our part in the two-way interaction with the Lord and His Spirit (Galatians 5:25).

The kind of two-way interaction that is possible with the Spirit of Christ is not completely unlike the experience we would have with someone when we live in the same house with that person every day. With God, we can either experience a personal relationship that includes His discipline, yet is very close, loving, rewarding and rejuvenating. Or we can experience a personal relationship with God, including His discipline, which is misunderstood, estranged, shallow and distant. We can also flip back and forth between those two experiences when we are not skilled at listening to His voice.

Regardless, God's discipline is ongoing because Satan's attacks are ongoing.

The reality of following Christ is that you must always be prepared, first and foremost, to fight yourself (your old self). This is the struggle described in Romans 7:15-21. It is a sign of Satan's attacks and manipulations against who we are in Christ. As such, these internal struggles we face are the premier battles we must fight in the spiritual war.

When you do what God tells you to do to change, He enables your new self to emerge victorious. But at the same time, your old self will be unfamiliar with the aspect of faith that, from your old self's point of view, involves uncertainty and is counterintuitive to your survival instincts (Ephesians 4:17-24). This is characteristic of spiritual warfare, which is why skillful, personal interaction with the Spirit is so crucial.

Discipline is a vital attribute for success in spiritual war. Spiritual warfare is even more real than any kind of war man has fought. It is appropriate to become trained in the strategies and tactics of *spiritual* warfare as they are being waged in your life. Recognizing Satan's strategies and tactics against your life comes with the experience of applying insights to real life. Creating and gaining that experience is part of the purpose of learning to interact with the Spirit within.

SATAN AND OUR OLD SELF-NATURE ARE INVOLVED IN THE SPIRITUAL WAR

The military terminology and themes which pervade the Scriptures are not coincidental, nor are they just a reflection of the times in which the Scriptures were written. References to military concepts are a reflection of the reality of the spiritual war going on through the ages. While the outcome is known and God will win, this knowledge is not to be mistaken for a declaration that, as a believer, you are to "lay down arms" and not examine your own life regularly (evaluating your part in the battles). Paradoxically, fighting the spiritual war as a Christian involves acting from a place of peace in your heart. This involves facing the inner struggles or fight between your old and new selves. Fighting the inner fight is your part of connecting with God to experience peace.

Peace is freedom from disquieting or oppressive thoughts and emotions.[1] As Christians, we are NOT to be at peace through selfish indifference to God. In other words, when living for the Lord is difficult, we may experience a false sense of peace by contenting ourselves with the idea that we are sinners doing our "best." That contentment is NOT the same as being at peace. Being at peace also does NOT mean we stop fighting against Satan's influences within us. To be clear, fighting against Satan is NOT primarily about fighting him in others by controlling or fixing others. Becoming skilled at transforming difficulties and struggles in our own hearts is essential to experiencing the peace of Christ during a spiritual battle. Being discipled beyond the elementary teachings of Christ is how we develop that skill.

Discipleship is about learning *how* to *recognize* when the fight is happening *within you*. Satan's deceptions often cause us to fail to realize when he is attacking because he is skilled at deception. Satan attacks *frequently*, but with the power of God through His Spirit's guidance and counsel, we can overcome Satan each time he attacks. So while God may be willing to give us the desires of our hearts (Psalms 37:4-6), the spiritual skill of recognizing your desires and of determining whether Satan or God gave them to you is a key part of discipleship beyond the elementary teachings of Christ. Being discipled helps us to

---

[1] Merriam-Webster, Inc: *Merriam-Webster's Collegiate Dictionary.* Eleventh ed. Springfield, Mass.: Merriam-Webster, Inc., 2003 *(Frederick C. Mish)*

overcome Satan's greatest, most deceptive tactic: causing us to deny that we must change when he attacks us.

When we think of Satan as a deceiver, it isn't just because he is a bad guy and because we know he is a bad guy. Satan is The Deceiver because he is like the career thief, the repeat offender that gets caught, but only on occasions. We can see that Satan is at work, but it is almost always *after* the fact, **particularly in our own lives**! We see Satan's work in others very easily, and we imagine we can turn that perceptive skill upon ourselves; *that* is his deception. We assume we see Satan's attacks as often as they occur; *that* can be part of his deception.

Satan doesn't need us to see his deception in order to feel appreciated as a "skilled deceiver." Frankly, Satan doesn't care what we think about him because his beef is with God. Satan really cares about resisting God; we are just pawns and fodder for Satan's purposes. Satan is actually most effective in accomplishing his work when his ways cause us to believe we are living well for God when in fact we aren't.

When you don't know for sure how to hear the voice of God in your heart, or you aren't consistent in exercising that ability, it is much easier for Satan to influence your actions. Satan, being an effective deceiver ensures you *won't* be thinking to yourself, "I'm leaning on my own understanding right now," or, "I'm being deceived here," even half of the time when Satan is at work IN YOU. Satan does well in making sure that, most of the time, you don't think, "I'm getting caught up in worldly things right now," or "I'm falling away from the Lord due to my busy life!" Without a consistent two-way interaction with the Spirit, the patterns of the old self become, and remain, habits that we exercise mostly UNconsciously. Without regularity in hearing the Spirit's guidance, consciously we intend to live for the Lord, but UNconsciously we follow the patterns of the world and our old selves.

The Purpose of Discipleship

However, when Satan is being successful and you are willing to change, you can come to feel something missing in your walk with Christ. That feeling of inner lack is the Spirit speaking to you and seeking to change some things in your life. When the Spirit is speaking you in that way, it is time once again to count some potential costs that may come with the corrections He seeks to make in you. If you are prepared to submit completely to the Lord, discipleship beyond the elementary teachings becomes possible and useful.

We (the authors) were both military men. We were not generals, but we were officers. We led other men, and we were also led. Our military experience has been helpful in understanding our own experiences of Satan's tactics, in understanding the reason why the Father sent His Spirit in Jesus' name, in understanding and appreciating general concepts applicable to the spiritual conduct of battle, in understanding how Satan seeks to exert his will, and how Satan seeks to deceive us as to his true intentions.

In *On War*, one of the most pivotal books written on the subject of war, Carl Von Clausewitz defines war as the following (underline added by authors):

> "Countless duels go to make up war, but a picture of it as a whole can be formed by imagining a pair of wrestlers. Each tries through physical force to compel the other to do his will; his immediate aim is to throw his opponent in order to make him incapable of further resistance. <u>War is thus an act of force to compel our enemy to do our will.</u>"[2]

---

[2] Michael Howard and Peter Paret, eds., *On War* by Carl Von Clausewitz, (Princeton University Press, 1989), pg. 75.

A Disciple's Heart

Isn't that exactly what the Scriptures say Satan seeks to do in us? Satan wants to render us incapable of resisting him as he seeks to compel us to do his will. Satan uses deception and illusion; he gets your attention focused outside of you at the very moment when your attention needs to be focused inside you. When we don't live as if Satan seeks to render us incapable of resisting his will, we may gain an unwarranted confidence in ourselves.

Similarly, in *The Art of War*, Sun Tzu says some things about the importance of knowing yourself, knowing your enemy, and the relationship of these to victory in warfare. They apply to the spiritual war. The following is a quote from that book. We (the authors) have added some spiritual distinctions in italics so that you might see the relevance.

"'Know the enemy *(Satan and old self)*, know yourself *(who you are in Christ)*,

And victory is never in doubt, not in a hundred battles.'

He who knows self *(who you are in Christ)* but not the enemy *(Satan and old self)*

Will suffer one defeat for every victory.

He who knows neither self *(who you are in Christ)* nor enemy *(Satan and old self)*

Will fail in every battle."[3]

A fairly common Christian view of spiritual warfare is similar, in a limited way, to the stereotypical concept of WWI.

---

[3] John Minford edited, translated and introduction, *The Art of War* by Sun-Tzu, (The Penguin Group, Penguin Books, 2002), pg. 19.

In WWI, there were clear lines between friendly and enemy forces. Both were entrenched on either side of an imaginary line. This line was called "The front line." Behind the front line most everything was safe; usually there was no enemy there. Forward of the front line was where the enemy was usually located.

In spiritual warfare there are *NO lines*. The enemy, Satan, attacks you from within! You may be able to see Satan's attacks in others, but it is not so easy when Satan attacks you. Those are the attacks the Holy Spirit will speak to you about first — the attacks on you. When Satan attacks, there is no safe place for you until you listen to the voice of the Spirit in your heart. When Satan attacks others, who in turn harm you, there may be no safe place outside of you, but if you listen to the voice of the Spirit in your heart, there will be a safe place within. That safe place is in the arms of the Lord who loves us, and with His Spirit who seeks to comfort us. Discipleship is about learning how to make the inner world real in terms of how you feel in the face of struggles.

To discover the various ways Satan attacks, we don't have to be military experts or read books on military matters. We do, however, need to be able to examine our lives to be able to identify how Satan wields his influences. Listening to God's voice requires being *willing* to discover Satan's subtle and gross attacks against us. When we recognize Satan's influences within us, we will begin to appreciate how God is disciplining us.

While the quotes and analogies above may be interesting and applicable, we cannot be victorious over Satan with someone else's information about God or about Satan. Our knowledge about spiritual war must come from our own *experience* of hearing God's voice intentionally coupled with a continual, personal examination of our lives and the study of God's written Word. Without the daily, direct experience of listening to the Spirit, our preconceived notions and assumptions can be what Satan uses to defeat us. This is true though we may study God's written Word diligently. Without also examining our experiences and our attempts to apply God's spoken and written Word to our lives, we may inadvertently separate God's Truth from His purpose for communicating it to us. This can happen without us being aware it is happening. It definitely happens when we cannot skillfully pay attention to our hearts.

God knows Satan better than Satan knows himself. The Spirit knows us better than we know ourselves. Therefore, when we rely on God's guidance by listening to His Spirit with our hearts, we can access His power, and God can direct us through the complexities Satan weaves. It all starts by recognizing our own real-life, specific application needs in fighting our spiritual battles. To draw on the help available in the Spirit, we must cultivate our part of the interaction with Him. Increasing our skill in that interactive relationship starts with something like the following attitude:

"There is more I need to learn from the Spirit. I may know some things, but what I know isn't solving all the problems I face. I may have some things, but what I have isn't consistent in creating peace for me. I may want some things, but I don't want my desires to drive me. I may have somebody, but others cannot complete me as a believer in Christ."

With that attitude, let's take a look at human teachers who disciple beyond the elementary teachings of Christ.

Chapter 2:

Going Beyond the Elementary Teachings with a Human Teacher

Growth Step 1:

To examine the human teacher discipleship environment and how it enables believers to hear God's voice with their own hearts.

Growth Step 2:

To understand how your assessment of your own growth needs will influence what you look for in a human teacher.

Growth Step 3:

To recognize and appreciate characteristics of the human teacher and the disciple of Christ, and how they facilitate spiritual growth in this discipleship environment.

The three discipleship environments each focus on developing and practicing three things: learning how to be equipped, skilled disciples of Christ; learning certain specific Scriptural skill sets; learning how to hear and listen to the Spirit with our hearts. While the human teacher discipleship environment involves learning, useful ways to learn to go beyond the elementary teachings of Christ are somewhat different than the approaches we typically use to learn the elementary teachings themselves. This chapter will highlight some of those differences.

While this chapter examines the human teacher discipleship environment, many of the goals and objectives in the discipleship environments of the human teacher and of fellowship for discipleship are similar. It is very easy to overlook key areas where they are similar because we have some "stereotypical views" of how we learn from human teachers or in fellowship with one another. Throughout the discussion, we will indicate where some of the less obvious similarities are.

Special Consideration:

As we talk about human teachers who help us go beyond the elementary teachings of Christ, bear the following in mind. The primary difference between the role of the Spirit as The Teacher and the role of a human teacher (other than the obvious) is that the Spirit (The Teacher) seeks to communicate to the disciple exactly *what* Satan's attack is, *what* change(s) the disciple must make to live in God's Truth in the moment, and *what* specific action(s) the disciple is to take to demonstrate faith in the moment. The human teacher's role is to help the disciple determine *how* to hear what the Spirit is saying. In short, the Spirit focuses on *what*, and the human teacher focuses on *how*.

There is much which involved in teaching the "how." The point in this discussion is to acknowledge those distinctions, **while being careful not to interpret them** as meaning the human teacher teaches something the Spirit cannot. The human teacher is simply a useful tool. This clarification is made because it honors the spiritual dynamics behind Jesus' purpose of telling the Disciples to go and make disciples (Matthew 28:19) as opposed to telling the Disciples to go inform the nations about Jesus. The Disciples were capable of teaching others the "how" because they were fully capable of being taught one-on-one from the Spirit (John 21:15-17). Paul was also capable of being taught one-on-one from the Spirit (1 Corinthians 2:6-10), though he had no physically human teacher.

KEY CONCEPT:

The Lord uses human teachers* to teach individual believers how to be discipled by the Spirit of God (Hebrews 5:11-14). Disciples of Christ may arrive at a place of spiritual growth where they are skilled in listening to the Spirit of God and are able to learn *directly* and consistently from the Spirit without a human teacher (1 John 2:26-27). The purpose of a human teacher,* cooperating with the guidance of the Spirit of God, is to assist a disciple of Christ in developing the ability to consistently listen to the Spirit of God through the heart *without* a human teacher.

<u>*1 John 2:27:*</u> "As for you, the anointing which you received from Him abides in you, and you have no need for anyone to teach you; but as His anointing teaches you about all things, and is true and is not a lie, and just as it has taught you, you abide in Him."

<u>*Hebrews 5:12:*</u> "For though by this time you ought to be teachers, you have need again for someone to teach you the elementary principles of the oracles of God, and you have come to need milk and not solid food."

* The purpose and aim of the human teacher and of that fellowship without the human teacher is actually the same, but the roles of believers being discipled within each are different.

We submit ourselves to church leaders' teachings and discussions about God, the Scriptures, and living for Christ, and we view that teaching as sufficient to enable us to apply the information we learn. Because we do learn some useful things from other believers pertaining to spiritual growth, we frequently come to conduct ourselves as though we do not need much specific help in hearing the Spirit's guidance pertaining to our "personal and private affairs." As a result, within a few years of choosing to follow Christ, we often come to think we do not need a human teacher to instruct us on specifically *how* to hear God direct our lives in terms of our personal affairs.

We often view ourselves as capable and being in charge of our own lives. We often consider the purpose of programs and activities in church as serving to remind us to do mostly what we already know to do, and thanking the Lord for what He has done for us. We view church as a place where we can participate in furthering the Lord's work by bringing others to Him. We view church as the place to be encouraged and lifted up as we handle our personal lives the way we believe God wants us to handle them. While fulfilling these purposes is indeed part of the functioning of the Body, those views reveal a key assumption which we are making: we already know how to hear the voice of God; we already know how to figure out what He wants of us.

1 John 2:27 is a verse many Christians claim for themselves after some period of church training and classes. Specifically, our lives demonstrate that we often claim the status of being skilled enough to hear the Spirit's counsel as regularly as He offers it.

To claim the status described in 1 John 2:27, we must be consistent in hearing the voice of God clearly, and be skilled both in understanding and following the specific directives He speaks to in our hearts. When we have these skills, our lives

A Disciple's Heart

demonstrate a godly understanding of the dynamics of the heart. If your Christian training has facilitated that for you, then you have been blessed and you could "insert" your name in place of "you" when you read 1 John 2:27.

But if a believer cannot honestly claim that status, then that believer does in fact have a need for one of the two discipleship environments involving fellow believers: being discipled by the Spirit through a human teacher; being discipled by the Spirit through a fellowship for discipleship. In those two discipleship environments, we can learn to submit our free will to the Lord so we may become skilled in being discipled directly from the Spirit through our hearts.

Free will gives us the God-given right to make choices for the Lord or according to Satan's influence, whether we recognize those choices or not. The choice to live for Christ is supposed to indicate we are interested in routinely examining the choices in our lives by developing the ability to deliberately hear the Spirit's guidance pertaining to them. The human teacher discipleship environment helps believers develop that skill in the company of a believer who already knows how to hear the Spirit clearly with the heart.

Hebrews 5:12 introduces the idea of various kinds of spiritual food. The milk versus solid food is a metaphor and implies there are various degrees of growth in one's walk with the Lord. This is one of several verses which, when misunderstood, seem to "permit" us to grow in our spiritual awareness in whatever ways that might come naturally to us. When misunderstood, both 1 John 2:27 and Hebrews 5:12 are among the verses that appear to permit us to "grow in our own time."

Hebrews is talking to people who are moving in a particular life direction because it is more familiar to them. Hebrews was written to Christian Jews who were tending to take their old lifestyle approach, which was based on Judaism, and integrating "following Christ" into that. When we have not learned how to hear and follow the voice of God, and to discover how to apply His spoken word to our lives, then the theme of the Hebrews message applies to us.

That Hebrews 5:12 might apply to us can be a real blow to our Christian pride as the verse is typically considered to be a warning not to "backslide." We usually think of "backsliders" as really bad Christians who do not care much about God. Our opinion of backsliders is that they are Christians, ensnared by Satan, who have little to no motivation to live for God, even in some of the most basic ways. We think they are Christians who live incorrectly because they no longer have the love of God as their first love.

While those concepts of "backsliders" may be true, such a limited view focuses our attention away from examining ourselves, because we usually do not think of ourselves as Christians who have gone to the extreme associated with "backsliding." This is a deceptive view. In Hebrews, the writer is talking to *believers* who needed a refresher on some basics *because* they were tending to integrate the new life into their old *familiar* ways, according to their own *desires* and *comfort* levels. This can be a warning to us, whose culture argues for and glorifies the virtues of individual freedoms and our rights to live life in whatever ways seem to come naturally to us and please us. Our culture's ways can easily become the means by which we deal with our troubles and woes, which actually indicate spiritual issues in our lives.

The writer of Hebrews tells the Christians they must move forward in their relationships with God and discusses how and why thoroughly. The writer was functioning as a human teacher who knew the recipients, though the "interaction" was limited due to having to write it in a letter.

The human teacher assists believers in discovering how to identify when and where we are being tempted. The human teacher shows us how to examine our lives and how to clearly identify Satan's attack on, and lies about, who we are in Christ.

WHAT IS THE PURPOSE OF THE HUMAN TEACHER?

The idea is NOT to get Christians lined up in the same uniform, looking like a bunch of pre-stamped spiritual soldiers whose lives are exactly the same — definitely not.

The human teacher's teaching does not point to himself and what he wants, but to the Spirit of Christ within the disciple. The human teacher functions to teach followers of Christ to follow *Christ* in life, both in and out of church. The human teacher functions to teach disciples of Christ how to live as disciples of Christ, by learning how to interact with and to learn from *The* Teacher: the Spirit of Christ, the Holy Spirit.

The ultimate goal of the human teacher discipleship environment is to assist disciples of Christ in becoming able to be discipled consistently and effectively, one-on-one with the Spirit and without the human teacher. In this way the human teacher seeks to "work himself out of his God-given job." But we must always remember that accomplishing that task is not entirely up to the Spirit and the human teacher. You, the disciple, are part of that equation as well.

It is not necessarily the Lord's intent that human teachers stand alone. The idea is that in being taught how to listen to the Spirit one-on-one, some disciples of Christ will be able to become human teachers capable of working with the Spirit to disciple others in learning from the Spirit one-on-one. Working with the Spirit to grow human teachers capable of discipling beyond the elementary teachings is critical to the vitality of the

Body of Christ as it increases in numbers. Unless other human teachers are grown, the tendency of the body is to lose the ability to focus on listening to the Spirit speaking to our individual real-life application issues, and to lose the kinds of spiritually intimate, personal interactions requisite to being discipled and to functioning as a body.

Some disciples of Christ who have grown in the Spirit through a human teacher may not be able to become teachers. Alternatively, based on God's plan for their lives, they may not have the time to commit to personally discipling others. Still, they are able to strongly support and encourage believers who are in the process of learning how to interact with the Spirit within. Disciples of Christ who no longer need a human teacher can strengthen the body by participating in fellowship for discipleship, and by helping lay the foundation for other believers to go beyond the elementary teachings of Christ.

In these general ways, the purpose of the human teacher is to work in support of The Teacher, the Spirit of God, to disciple other disciples of Christ. The human teacher points to Christ and the Spirit given to believers as a result of His sacrifice. The purpose of the human teacher is to do his part to support continual growth, which comes from going beyond the elementary teachings of Christ and builds up a stronger Body of Christ.

Why Is a Personal Relationship with the Human Teacher So Important in This Discipleship Environment?

Being born into the world, we are all born into sin. We have sinful origins whether we have accepted salvation or not. Salvation does not eliminate the existence of our sinful origins; salvation cleanses us from sin. Salvation does not physically prevent us from taking a sinful action; salvation enables us to learn to interact with the Spirit and be shown how not to act sinfully, even concerning areas of life where the Scriptures are silent.

These concepts indicate that the role of the human teacher includes helping the disciple to recognize his old self routinely and to develop a detachment toward his old self. To help in that way, the human teacher must know something of the life of the disciple. Without a personal relationship with the disciple, teachings would be limited to more general and broad applications. Paul's letter to the Romans is an example of this and stands out in contrast to the letters he wrote to believers whose lives he was more familiar with. The letter to the Romans is considered one of the best and most comprehensive explanations of many elementary teachings of Christ.

In discipling, the human teacher often draws on his own recent and current experiences in fighting Satan's influence by listening to the Spirit of God in order to demonstrate *how* it is done. The human teacher often challenges the disciple's rationale by highlighting inconsistencies in his listening. The human teacher often addresses a disciple's inconsistencies in listening by showing how the actions are inconsistent with the elementary kinds of teachings. Those inconsistencies are often revealed by the condition of the disciple's heart and how he is applying the principles governing how to hear the Spirit, which are demonstrated in the Scriptures themselves. These interactions between the human teacher and the disciple of Christ are, however, different from telling the disciple what God is actually saying to him.

We have a strong sense of identity with the old self NOT because we *consciously* desire what our old self desires, **but because we, most often, unconsciously desire what our old self wants.** Satan, of course, is behind the drive of our old selves. Listening to the Spirit of God with the heart is what enables us to become consciously aware of Satan's influence and our old selves. The purpose of becoming aware is so that we may actively participate in the spiritual war within us, and avoid sinning due to being unaware!

The personal relationship between the human teacher and disciple of Christ enable them to focus together on real-life experiences of the spiritual war. 1 John 3:18-24 tells us it is our hearts which condemn us, and only if our hearts do not condemn us can we have confidence before God. If the heart is not filled with peace and love, then we are being warned that we are under attack by Satan. The warning is part of the work of the Holy Spirit within us. In Colossians 3:5-11, Paul says we are to kill our earthly natures by ridding ourselves of a whole variety of emotions, including anger, malice, etc. Yet in Ephesians 4:26 Paul indicates we can experience anger without sinning. Finally, in Genesis 4:6-7, the Lord tells Cain that when he is experiencing disturbances in his heart, sin wants him and is lying in wait for him; he must master it. Take a moment to examine the group of verses mentioned in this paragraph, and then continue.

The personal relationship with the human teacher facilitates discussion and evaluation of the disciple's heart disturbances. When a believer experiences a disturbance in his heart, the Spirit is speaking to make a change in that believer. When we experienced the change of heart in our salvation experience, we *interacted* in some way so that we heard the Spirit. We don't often focus on how we heard the voice of the Spirit with our hearts. We focus on how we heard with our minds. Similarly, the verses in the paragraph above indicate the Spirit is speaking to our hearts at other times when we experience various kinds of heart conditions.

When Satan attacks us, Satan is using a situation in our life to

A Disciple's Heart

tempt us — sin wants us. The Spirit sees we are in trouble and He immediately begins speaking in our hearts. As in salvation, we can come to "hear" the Spirit tell us what we must do to avoid sin. In so doing, we experience a transformation in our hearts. Without a personal relationship with the human teacher, the disciple is sometimes not challenged to identify these opportunities, nor is he consistently able to capitalize on them.

The personal relationship enables the human teacher to assist a disciple of Christ in recognizing the voice of the Spirit of his/her Master, Christ. The human teacher assists the disciple in developing an appreciation and insightfulness into what often appears as insignificant, normal experiences of mild discomfort, stress, or concern. Sometimes the human teacher and disciple of Christ work together during a trial, and sometimes the application examinations are after the fact. The human teacher does not have to be present when a heart disturbance is happening, but for a disciple of Christ to learn how to apply God's truth, events *must* be felt and examined. The personal relationship and interaction between the human teacher and the disciple of Christ facilitates learning from these opportunities.

When the disciple accepts the importance of discussing actual events in his life, the human teacher and disciple(s) can move out of "theory," or mental information, and into everyday reality. This is when the tentacles of the old self really become revealed and can be changed. The nature of the old self is to function to influence the heart in certain predictable ways according to patterns created uniquely by a believer's perception of his life experiences. Those patterns become learning tools when they can be identified. Through the personal relationship between human teacher and disciple of Christ, the disciple learns to recognize those patterns with consistency and regularity whenever they come into play in a life situation. Observing the patterns is helpful in determining how to recognize Satan's attacks, and in differentiating the Spirit's voice during times of inner conflict.

For these reasons, the personal relationship between the human teacher and the disciple of Christ includes:

1. Identifying the daily influences of the disciple's sinful origins in practical, real-life terms.
2. Identifying Satan's activity and motives behind those influences.
3. Recognizing when the disciple's heart points to *spiritually intended conflicts* with his mind.
4. Helping the disciple to hear the Spirit's guidance through the heart in those real-life situations.
5. Helping the disciple to interact with the Spirit and transform pain to peace during the trial.
6. Emphasizing confidentiality among the disciples.
7. Emphasizing honesty and openness among the disciples.
8. Emphasizing consistency in practice, prayer, worship, and in relationships.
9. Emphasizing a solid examination of the Scriptures in both study and practice.

The phrase "spiritually intended conflicts" (from number 3 above) simply means there are conflicts within us of which we are supposed to be aware. Galatians 5:16-18 mentions these conflicts, as does Romans 7:15-21. They are conflicts within us between our old and new selves. They are conflicts between the Spirit's guidance and the desires of our old selves. We are supposed to be aware of these inner conflicts. When we *are* aware, we feel it. We usually don't feel joyful (Hebrews 12:11).

Once we are aware, we can focus on learning to change and transform. Because being aware of spiritually intended conflicts isn't comfortable, we usually distract ourselves from the feelings that point to those conflicts. The personal relationship seeks to strengthen the disciple's resolve to avoid short-term coping mechanisms by focusing on regular interaction and transformation with the Spirit.

The idea that we experience inner conflicts of which we must be aware reflects the fact that spiritual warfare is not about the absence of inner conflict. It is about the transformation of inner conflict. Peace works in relationship to spiritually intended conflicts. That relationship enables peace to *potentially* guard our hearts and minds (Philippians 4:7). When we learn *how* to *let* peace guard our hearts and minds, it will guard them; this does not happen automatically (Colossians 3:15; Philippians 4:7). You must participate with the Spirit of peace.

The personal relationship focuses on honesty of the new self. We usually want to avoid looking at some heart disturbances so much that we may begin to deny to ourselves when they are happening. But when our inner sense of peace is gone, it indicates when the disturbances are happening. To some extent we are usually aware of that, unless we are in full denial, quenching the Spirit fully in a given situation. Becoming aware is nurtured consistently through the personal relationship with the human teacher. Our inner disturbances are flags indicating that we must focus on passing away or transforming our old selves by hearing the Spirit's counsel in those moments. This is because in the moments we experience the disturbances, our old selves are seeking to assert themselves within us.

The relationship between the human teacher and the disciple of Christ emphasizes that we are not supposed to stop looking for the activity of Satan and our old selves simply because we are believers and are forgiven. We must learn how to be on guard, readily able to identify spiritually intended conflicts, so we do not act in sin without even noticing. Awareness of inner conflicts permits transformation during a trial (Romans 5:3-5). It is how we permit, or allow, the peace of Christ to rule in our hearts (Colossians 3:15). It is what enables us to know when it is time to focus on the Spirit's guidance in our hearts.

The personal relationship between the human teacher and the disciple of Christ facilitates awareness of the spiritual war, as it unfolds within the disciple. Spiritual warfare is about skillfully paying attention to internal conflict and transforming it to peace by following Christ each time His Spirit warns our hearts. The personal relationship supports learning how to listen to the Spirit of Christ in one's heart and on dragging those inner conflicts out in the open to destroy them with God's Truth about who we are in Christ. Without well-developed transformation skills, we will typically act specifically and sinfully in ways that actually avoid heart disturbances. Without well-developed transformation skills, we typically seek to bring pains to an end in ways we do not recognize serve Satan. The personal relationship supports the disciple in developing those transformation skills necessary to effectively fight in the spiritual war.

The personal relationship helps disciples to develop the power of pause. The inner, spiritually intended conflicts indicate when our fleshly origins are seeking to preserve or assert themselves and increase their power over our new selves in Christ. **Many times when we do not notice spiritually intended conflicts within, it is because we do not pause to question our desires before we fulfill them. Because we have *reasons* to fulfill our desires, *we think we actually are* questioning the desires themselves.**

We often fail to pause to seek out the Spirit's lessons (Lord's discipline) contained in our experiences. Because we are mostly acquainted with the experiences we have with our five senses and our minds, the spiritual lessons of the heart are much more difficult to notice, to appreciate and to value. The spiritual lessons of the heart are completely minimized by our worldly culture mostly because they are very difficult to quantify and measure. To the physical world, the heart is "outside the box." For these reasons, it is sometimes hard for us to consistently receive the Spirit's guidance and counsel. The five senses normally do not experience that interaction, and the Spirit's guidance/counsel does not make any sense to the mind of the old self. In that case, the disciple's personal relationship with the human teacher functions largely to draw attention to those spiritual lessons in the heart so the disciple can learn to routinely identify the spiritually intended conflicts for himself. That relationship is to demonstrate how to love the Lord in daily life so that the requisite transformation of pain (examples listed on page 20) becomes not only possible but also routine.

How Do We Cultivate Detachment Toward Our Old Selves and Why?

Today people understand the meaning of the phrase "knowledge is power." We place great value on all forms of education and often set minimum standards of learning for children in school. We do the same with our approach to learning how to live for God. But when it comes to living for God, **it is only when the heart is changed that we gain a true knowledge of God's Truth.** Change happens in conjunction with application to real-life issues on a *reoccurring* basis. This principle applies to how we pass away or kill the old self whenever it surfaces in our life experiences.

Application (living) of God's Truth requires faith. Faith requires a change of heart in the midst of uncertainty of the future. This is different from being uncertain about what God wants you to do in a specific situation. Faith requires a change of heart in the midst of undesirable situations which may include times when God's direction for you is undesirable to your old self. Remember, you are being challenged to hear the Spirit, transform and have faith to act differently when you feel the feelings listed on page 20.

Scriptural knowledge itself is critical, but alone it is insufficient to precipitate a change of heart. The Pharisees and Judas are clear examples of Scripturally knowledgeable people who did not experience a change of heart, though we usually do not see them as being like us. Some other examples where knowledge was not sufficient to precipitate a change of heart are: Abram (Genesis 12:1-20); David (2 Samuel 11:1-27); Peter (Matthew 26:69-75); Martha (Luke 10:38-42); Thomas (John 20:24-29); Ananias and Sapphira (Acts 5:1-11).

To precipitate a change of heart, we must recognize *when* it must change. We must first recognize when our old selves are seeking to assert themselves, then we must seek out the changes the Lord seeks in us. For these reasons, the human teacher focuses on recognizing when the Spirit is speaking, so we *can* cultivate detachment from our old selves.

Detachment deals with seeing our old selves regularly so we can listen to the Spirit tell us how to act in our new selves. Detachment from one's old self does not happen by ignoring or trying to push the old self away. Detachment happens by recognizing what the old self wants, by learning how to listen to the Lord tell us how to change the old self's desire, and by hearing God's Spirit tell us how specifically to act in the new self. **To develop detachment from our old selves, we must learn to hate certain things at certain times.** This kind of hate is not the old self-fulfilling sort of "I'm right and you're wrong" hate, it is the kind of hate that comes with a stronger love for the

Lord (Luke 14:26-27).

The kind of hate that comes from a stronger love for the Lord is only possible when we actually hear and accept the Lord's specific changes for us, which are expressed by His Spirit in our hearts when they are disturbed. Without that listening skill, we tend to determine what is right on an "absolute basis." In other words, we know that family is a good thing. It would seem to follow that whatever preserves relationships in the family would be what God wants. However, there are times when the things we do to preserve family relationships result in causing us to diminish who we are in Christ. This is often a difficult distinction to make, but the Spirit speaks to it when it is happening or about to happen. Let's look more at how those love/hate dynamics may play out in family relationships. Realize that these dynamics can happen in any situation concerning not only relationships, but also lifestyles, living conditions, and preferences.

There are times when we fear standing up for what the Lord would have us to stand up for because that stand could cause trouble within family relationships. Fearing instability, insecurity, and being alone are among the inner experiences which may characterize such situations. Regardless, when these times arise, we will usually feel some level of discomfort. Sometimes when these situations arise we will feel pleasure, not because we are happy about potential family disharmony, but because we are happy to do what will make other family members happy. There is nothing inherently wrong with that. But when our old selves might seek to make family happy at the expense of listening to God, we can feel the voice of God in our hearts because our hearts will be disturbed. When this happens, it does NOT follow that whatever it is you think at the time is what God wants you to think! No, listening to God is critical to determine the content of the Spirit's counsel to you.

It is during such times that being discipled beyond the elementary teachings of Christ enables you to identify Satan's attack on you, to discover the change(s) the Lord wishes you to make in you, and to hear how the Lord wants you to handle things. If, when seeking to do God's will, you incorrectly believe that doing God's will for you is going to cause everyone else to get along with you and be continually and lovingly supportive of you, then you are mistaken. The interpersonal dynamics between someone who can hear and listen to God well and family members who cannot can cause distance within families. When you listen and follow the Spirit, you may sometimes be making a stand at times when others may not understand why. Others may accuse you of being quite hypocritical. Matthew 10:34-36 expresses this dynamic very clearly.

Hearing the Spirit well and *intending* to hear Him well are two *very* different things. Satan wants us to have difficulty hearing the Lord or to question whether it is even possible sometimes. By standing up for something *without* being able to hear God clearly and accurately for yourself with your heart, you may actually make mistakes and sin, regardless of your good intentions. It takes skill to hear the voice of God and to properly live in peace and love while properly demonstrating hate and detachment to one's old self desires. The human teacher functions to help disciples of Christ to skillfully double-check what they believe the Spirit is saying, so they may minimize potential mistakes in listening to the Spirit.

Matthew 8:21-22 reflects the same theme about being willing to listen to God and accept the reprioritization that He will require in your life. In this passage, a disciple seeks Jesus' support for what the world considers a very important and emotional occasion: a funeral of one's parent. Jesus is not saying that to live for God we must stop attending funerals. Skipping the funeral was one of the "real-life" applications for that particular disciple at that particular time.

Some believers are of the opinion that the disciple's parent was not actually dead and that the disciple was simply seeing how Jesus would respond to the issue. Regardless, the issue of counting the cost of being discipled would not be irrelevant even if the parent were not dead. Jesus is saying that when He is directing us to do something, whatever excuse we may find to wait to fulfill His will in that moment is inappropriate. Whatever may cause us to wait is the very thing we will be challenged to give up. Jesus is saying that even when a task in the service of God is conflicting with something very personal and meaningful, then regardless how "right" our other desire seems to be, we must be willing to place the priority on what God is telling and has told us to do.

Depending on Satan's attacks, our circumstances, and our heart dynamics, God's course of action for us concerning the attendance of a funeral could be different. Depending on one's family, not attending a funeral could cause significant family repercussions and could even be interpreted as being indifferent and "unchristian." But when Jesus physically departed this earth, the Father gave us His Spirit to tell us when these sorts of occasions arise in our lives today. The Spirit offers us counsel, direction and guidance and can teach us how to apply these truths to the unique circumstances of our lives. While we do not know how the disciple in Matthew 8:21-22 responded, we can disregard the Spirit's voice just like the rich young man actually did (Mark 10:17-31). Similarly, we may walk away from the direction the Lord seeks to lead us in because we do not understand His direction or intentions (John 6:60-66). Conflicting priorities and desires mean the recognition of, and detachment from, our old selves is a critical skill for us to learn.

Jesus gives another example of the hate/love dynamics involved in detachment to the old self when He addresses the issue of possessions and treasures. Matthew 6:19-24 indicate that listening to and following the Lord's directives for your life will often require you to make difficult choices in terms of what you treasure. Jesus says we are to trust Him and know what He wants of us even when Satan tries to fill us with fear concerning our very ability to survive (Matthew 6:25-34). We must learn to hate the drives in us that cause us to fear fulfilling His will for us. Knowing His specific will for you and following it is part of carrying your own cross (Luke 14:27).

The point of the passages dealing with the costs of being His disciple are not provided by the Scriptures in order that you hate your relatives for no reason or to get rid of your possessions "just because." The point is that you must be *prepared* to give up whatever is dear to you in order to follow Christ as God's Spirit directs. Again, **you need to know what He wants you to do, how He wants it done, and why! Hearing and doing God's will sometimes requires you to change your life in ways that may alienate you from using the things people often lean on to comfort themselves as a substitute for listening to God.** Luke 9:23-26 and Luke 14:25-33 indicate that if a person who claims to follow Christ does not take into account the cost potentially required, then failure will result and, in a moment when it counts, the believer will turn his back on the Lord's will through his actions.

Jesus says we are to love one another as He has loved us (John 13:35, 15:12). The human teacher/disciple relationship helps the disciple to understand how it is we can love one another yet be doing things that "cause" others to feel very painful feelings (their own heart disturbances) toward our actions. The human teacher/disciple relationship enables the disciple to hear the Spirit and properly apply all of God's Truth that is contained in seemingly contrary statements as "Honor your mother and father" (Deuteronomy 5:16), "hate your father and mother and wife and children and brothers and sisters" (Luke 14:26), yet "love your enemies" (Luke 6:27) and "do not judge and do not condemn" (Luke 6:37). The human teacher/disciple relationship teaches how to listen to the voice of God clearly and consistently so that we don't worry about our lives (Luke 12:22), yet to be able to ask whatever we wish (knowing whether to ask for possessions, money, security, a partner, etc.) and have it done for us (John 15:7), while not contradicting Luke 14:33, which says we must give up all our possessions.

Discerning the real-life applications you are being directed to demonstrate means knowing for sure when the Spirit is counseling you to give up or hold on to something. It requires practicing attachment toward the new self and detachment toward the old self.

WHAT CONSTITUTES THE LESSONS A DISCIPLE RECEIVES FROM THE HUMAN TEACHER?

In general, neither the human teacher nor disciple picks the lessons. God provides them depending on when and where Satan attacks. The Spirit points out the relevant lessons clearly, and in hearing well, the human teacher and disciple can discover the lessons contained in whatever is going on in the disciple's life at the time.

The lessons are directly related to all the life struggles a disciple faces, big or small. The human teacher can often see where the lessons are when the disciple can't quite see the forest for the trees. The human teacher will sometimes point lessons out and suggest where the disciple should place his or her energy and learning efforts. In other words, the human teacher points to the Spirit speaking to the Lord's discipline in the disciple's life. Without this assistance, a believer can easily misinterpret much of the Lord's discipline as being mostly about things he cannot control: death, "acts of God," unforeseen disasters, bad things someone else did, etc.

We usually think that some issues and discomforts are just a "normal" part of living life in a sinful world. We routinely do not see how potentially viable options and "coincidence" also frequently relate to the Lord's discipline. Hearing His Spirit clearly is required so that if and when desirable options and coincidental events arise, which may be parts of the Lord's discipline, we can recognize Satan's temptation. Satan's temptations often cause us to take action on seemingly fortuitous options or to act on "coincidental" events in ways that contradict the direction the Spirit has already been giving. We often inadvertently feed the desires of our old selves by assuming fortuitous events are of God. Believers can easily fail to recognize the actual temptation contained within these kinds of life situations.

The disciple's lessons fundamentally deal with temptation arising from the lusts and desires within his own heart (James 1:13-15). Often Satan achieves his purposes by allowing us to recognize an obvious temptation, while his true aim is to divert our attention from the not-so-obvious-part of the temptation he wants us to fall for. So we will see the stone we might trip on, and while we are focused on the stone and cautiously stepping past it, we continue walking, but in a different direction than what God intends. This is the self-appointed job which Satan is good at: deception.

Satan isn't always so blatant as to cause us to live wicked lives. Satan offers "good" things, just like he offered to meet Jesus' basic survival needs (Matthew 4:3), offered to meet Jesus' security and safety needs (Matthew 4:5-6), and offered to give Jesus a comfortable lifestyle (Matthew 4:8-9). Had Jesus accepted those "good" things and not seen through the temptations, Jesus'

A Disciple's Heart

actions would have been sin. The human teacher helps the disciples to interact with the Spirit to cultivate the skill of seeing a temptation when it is disguised by "good" things.

Many Western Christians think that having certain needs met in the fashion we see in others' lives around us (in ways that focus on attaining a particular lifestyle) is what God wants for us AND is the way believers are supposed to live! This could be a legitimate viewpoint were the world without sin. But now, due to the nature of the fallen world, that isn't always the case. God provides security, comfort, and safety, but not necessarily in the ways of the world.

As a result of listening to the Spirit of Christ within, the disciple's actions may often be visibly different from the results which non-Christians experience. The disciple learns to be peaceful and content in experiencing more with less, whenever this is how the Spirit's counsel indicates it must be. When he does have more, the disciple learns to submit to the Spirit and be cautious, seeking to maintain the attitude of a steward, not an owner.

The Lord asks us to serve Him in the way He directs, not in the way our old, worldly selves are used to. Disciples will discover that dealing with normal issues and discomforts isn't supposed to involve the approach of "if it works out that I can get this or do that then it is the Lord's will." That view causes us to think that things which happen and appear good to us *are* usually from the Lord and for the taking, and that isn't always true. However, that is the kind of approach we often use when we have a need to know how to consistently listen to God speaking, and it seriously overlooks the significant role Satan plays against believers he wants to weaken.

The goal of the disciple's lessons is to learn to listen to God speaking specifically to him and *knowing for sure* what the Spirit is saying. Being a disciple isn't about living a life with a lot of question marks. It is about getting need-to-know answers when we need to know them. The ability to get solid, detailed answers from the Spirit is part of a blessing we may experience as disciples of Christ. But the flipside of being a disciple of Christ is about learning how to deal with the old self when the old self doesn't like God's answer!

The disciple discovers that many real-life issues are filled with messages from the Spirit through the heart, and those messages are about the various ways God intends for the disciple to change. So, the human teacher doesn't always give away lots of answers. The human teacher knows the point is for the disciple to connect with The Teacher within. The human teacher helps, but challenges the disciple to figure out the answers the Spirit provides in real-life experience. These interactions lead to wisdom of the Spirit and a skillful ability to apply Scriptural truth to everyday life situations.

The human teacher continually points out that when uncomfortable situations arise, there is something to learn. The disciple learns to ask more questions and make fewer statements. Questions reveal a seeking attitude. Still, the quality of questions isn't always the same. Questions must be useful and from the heart. When the disciple asks questions, the human teacher knows when to answer the question directly and knows when the disciple needs to question his question to see what is underneath it. This wisdom ensures the human teacher doesn't rob the disciple of learning the lesson, which is really between the disciple and the Lord he loves.

Examining and understanding Scripture is often a part of the disciple's lessons. While the divine nature of the elementary teachings of Christ can come alive in light of application in the Spirit, usually there are multiple Scriptures which can apply to a particular situation. The human teacher teaches the disciple how to listen to the heart in order to determine which of those Scriptures the Spirit is saying is most appropriate to a given situation. The lessons in discipleship involve an examination of the Scriptures, but, as mentioned in Chapter 1, it isn't just a Bible study. Real-life experiences, and the lessons in them, are examined in light of the Scriptures, in light of God's design of the dynamics of the heart, and in light of the Scriptural principles governing how to hear the voice of God.

Due to the unique lessons God gives to each disciple according to his own true needs, disciples of Christ may each experience the human teacher and the lessons somewhat differently (1 Corinthians 2:14-3:2; Galatians 3:1-5; Ephesians 1:15-17). This is, in part, because each disciple is a unique person created by God. It is also because an aspect of a person's uniqueness, which is NOT God-created, is the result of the disciple's conscious and unconscious cooperation with the will of Satan. (Compare 1 Corinthians 4:17-21 to 2 Timothy 1:15; compare Peter's fear in Matthew 26:69-74 to Thomas' doubt in John 20:24-25 to Judas betrayal in Luke 22:47-48.)

Because we have all done things Satan wanted us to do in our lives, we have unwittingly participated in weaving a web which is, at its essence, spiritual in nature. As we have discussed, this web forms patterns. The human teacher's job is to help the disciple observe those patterns (Romans 8:5-8, 12:2) as part of the lessons in learning how to hear the Spirit's voice.

How Is the Lord's Discipline a Discipleship Lesson?

While we touched on the Lord's discipline, it is worth considering a bit further. One of the first lessons in being discipled deals with one's own views of the Lord's discipline.

This is a foundational lesson. When we come to acknowledge that we often feel the kinds of feelings listed on page 20 whenever the Lord is disciplining us, then we begin to become aware of how important it is to notice how we feel. We become responsible to feel changes in our hearts and to own our part of working with the Spirit to transform those emotional pains to peace.

Appreciating the significance of the Lord's discipline is a foundational lesson because, while each disciple experiences disturbances of the heart differently, there are some very distinct differences and implications between men who experience emotional heart disturbances and women who experience them. Men are typically trained to suppress, hide, ignore, or disregard emotional experiences (heart disturbances) because they are considered signs of weakness. It is usually more acceptable for women to express or display certain emotions except, increasingly, in the workplace. Lessons in the purpose and principles behind the Lord's discipline are key to living effectively as disciples of Christ in order to understand the spiritual nature of emotional disturbances. Without those lessons, we often try to manage emotional disturbances and miss the opportunity to intentionally work with the Spirit during them.

Regardless of the stereotypical views of emotional experiences, and our culture's views on those who display them and when, acknowledging and working with heart disturbances is spiritually vital. The inability to interact with the Spirit during emotional situations does actually result in extremely poor decision making. This is often true not only from the world's point of view but also from the point of view of God and His Spirit! Everyone knows that a person who is "emotional" doesn't usually "think straight." This is part of God's design of the human being. Understanding why He designed us this way

A Disciple's Heart

is the purpose of receiving training in the dynamics of the heart and mind (one of the essentials discussed on page 42). As believers, we are supposed to understand the relationships between the Lord's discipline and the emotional and emotive content of life.

When we feel the emotions, which often comprise our heart's disturbances, we can learn to acknowledge that there is a reason of a spiritual nature. The Lord is seeking to do something in us. So when an uncomfortable situation arises, even though we may see someone else's contribution to our discomfort, we realize we are being disciplined by the Lord through the situation. This is when important questions may arise. What is the Lord trying to change in me? What is the Spirit saying to me? These are the kinds of questions that can motivate us to really put forth a skillful effort to fulfill our need to learn to hear the Spirit's voice. A believer's love for the Lord is reflected when those questions are asked, even if the believer has yet to obtain the answers. This is because acknowledging those questions cultivates the desire to seek to be discipled beyond the elementary teachings of Christ.

Being a disciple of Christ involves paying attention to your life. Just because you are living your life that does NOT mean you are paying attention to it. As we discussed, our lives are filled with patterns that repeat over and over due to Satan's success in getting us to do what he wants. They repeat and correspond to our failure to consistently hear the Lord speaking to us when our hearts are disturbed, i.e. those patterns are formed by our actions during emotionally uncomfortable life situations. There are big patterns and little patterns, and they often overlap in various ways. We usually recognize bits and pieces of the patterns at various times in our lives. But a skillful examination of the patterns of one's life is vital to recognizing when, where, how and why the Lord has been seeking to disciple us. This is essential to regularly experiencing the loving gratitude we can come to feel as a result of the Lord's discipline (1 Thessalonians 5:18).

The problem of correctly identifying the Lord's discipline can seem perplexing, complex and difficult to understand. This is because the Lord's discipline doesn't only deal with what we must change. The Lord's discipline also involves trying to get our attention and teach us how to hear Him. The problem is circular. Without being able to hear His voice consistently, you don't learn from the tests of His actual lessons contained in His disciplines. Without learning from the actual lessons in His discipline, you can't hear His voice consistently. Without hearing His voice, you don't hear the lesson, etc. That circular dynamic is what happens when Satan is deceiving us. Helping us to recognize our patterns and to break out of that circular dynamic is one reason why the Lord uses other believers as part of His "discipleship plan" — discipleship through a human teacher; fellowship for discipleship.

Is your ability to hear the Spirit's voice is so well developed that if the Lord spoke to your heart without using words, you would know if He was telling you to give up something dear to you voluntarily? The Scriptures indicate this skill is needed for many life situations when we are being disciplined by God (1 Corinthians 6:1-11, the right to sue in the judicial system; Philemon, Onesimus could have escaped slavery; Acts 5:1-11, Ananias and Sapphira held back on "voluntary" giving). Is your ability to hear with the heart so well developed that you could hear Him say anything which might be uncomfortable to you? Do you think you would know you had heard the Spirit's voice because you would consistently *want* to do something He asks that comes with a price for you to pay? Do you think you would know you had heard the Lord's voice because you would all of a sudden be *willing* to do it without having to transform

A Disciple's Heart

anything inside?

If you think that wanting to do God's will and being willing to do God's will are the criteria for determining whether or not God told you to do something, then you are making a grave error. That criterion means that when you do not want to do something or are not willing to do something, then it is because God does not want you to do that thing. This kind of thinking is an over-inflated view of the self because it assumes that you are completely the new self in Christ and are without an old self. This is the same as saying, "What I want is mostly what God's will actually is." That is the same as saying you are near perfect. That kind of thinking assumes God will change your wants and desires automatically. That kind of thinking can cause believers to distort what they think the Spirit is saying. Without an accurate understanding of the Lord's discipline, a believer will be hard pressed to skillfully compare his wants and desires to the patterns in Satan's attacks, and in the Spirit's previous guidance. This lack of spiritual skill decreases a disciple's ability to double-check for self-honesty. Being discipled beyond the elementary teachings of Christ helps believers to recognize and overcome this kind of thinking.

Psalms 37:4 (John 15:7 is also similar) says the Lord will give us the desires in our hearts only when we delight ourselves "in Him." But Hebrews 12:4-11 brings us back to reality by reminding us that being "in Him" means accepting His discipline, which is not usually pleasant.

To correct our thinking that causes us to believe our wants and desires are usually synonymous with God's will, we must accept that when God is disciplining us and speaking to us, we often *don't* want to do what He says (Hebrews 12:25). Being discipled helps us to recognize and understand that. When we are actually learning how to hear God's voice, our old selves will not like to hear what He is saying. When a disciple of Christ seeks to learn to hear His Spirit's voice anyway, that provokes a strong fight between the old and new selves. Jesus intends for His followers to be discipled in the company of believers because that internal fight is often very discombobulating, confusing, and challenging. We often need support we can audibly hear when we are learning to be discipled by the Spirit of Christ; audible support comes mostly from like-minded believers. The Spirit's voice is mostly inaudible. The human teacher is available to the disciple and is skilled, not only in teaching matters of the Spirit that precipitate the disciple's need for support, but also in providing that support whenever the disciple is in need of it.

Satan will routinely try to discourage a believer that seeks to cultivate a skillful two-way interaction with God. Satan does not want us to hear the Spirit well. Satan seeks to content us with solid Scriptural knowledge coupled with intermittent success in hearing the Spirit and rudimentary abilities to apply the divine Truth to our lives (Ephesians 5:1-2; Hebrews 6:12). Satan seeks to content us with the idea that skillful, personal interaction with the Spirit requires many years to learn. Unfortunately, it does often take many years to learn how to hear the Spirit's voice *without* being discipled beyond the elementary teachings of Christ in one of the environments that include fellow believers.

While we have a new self in Christ, we typically remain more comfortable with the old self. This is because Satan, via our own old selves, is a skilled false teacher lulling us into contentment with our past victories in Christ. As a skilled false teacher, Satan often deceives believers who have correct doctrinal knowledge so they apply that knowledge improperly and subtly. In the years without being discipled beyond the elementary teachings of Christ, a believer can miss many of the lessons in the Lord's discipline which are specific to himself.

Most of those lessons will repeat by simply involving different people at different times and in different places but with the same old heart conditions.

The spiritual skill of hearing the Spirit's voice consistently is NOT a gift that is given automatically to a believer. This is because of God's intention that we *must* exercise free will. In being discipled, we can develop a powerful ability to see that when the Lord is disciplining us, Satan is also attacking and our old selves are at work. This is one of the vital preparatory lessons in being discipled with a human teacher.

IS THERE A DIFFERENCE BETWEEN BEING A STUDENT OF CHRIST AND BEING A DISCIPLE OF CHRIST?

There are some very distinct differences between the student and the disciple. This distinction is worth a bit of extra attention. A disciple is in part a good student, but a good student is not necessarily a good disciple. The disciple of Christ realizes that mental knowledge alone does not change the heart. The disciple understands that the heart reveals what the mind has actually learned (Matthew 15:16-19). The disciple of Christ seeks to examine his heart in daily life situations to determine where the mental knowledge has not actually taken hold.

Earlier our discussions acknowledged that the beginning of discipleship involves learning the elementary teachings of Christ. The beginning of discipleship involves learning in the way a student learns, i.e. by acquiring mental knowledge and some application training. It is true that as disciples, we are always learning more about the teachings of Christ, so in a certain sense, a disciple is a student of his Master, Christ Jesus. However, being a good lifelong student of the Scriptures is not the totality of being a disciple. Discipleship environments directly assist disciples in going beyond the skillful acquisition of knowledge to become skillful in living that knowledge.

The disciple of Christ recognizes that it was not information which prompted the desire to live for Christ. The disciple of Christ realizes it was a change of heart in response to the Spirit that permitted the mind to accept the information which led to embracing salvation: information which pointed out failure and required change. We found salvation not through the steps which outline salvation, but by embracing the first of many changes described by the steps that led to salvation. In accepting His change in us, we accomplished the steps themselves.

The student of Christ focuses on the steps of salvation because they speak to change. That isn't inherently wrong. But there is a subtle and important difference between that and, after choosing to follow Christ, focusing on learning how the change occurred in the heart. Learning how change occurs in the heart is a skill. The skill must be applied regularly to hear the Spirit regularly and to be able to continually pass away the old self (2 Corinthians 5:17). This skill enables the disciple to continually interact with the Spirit whenever more change is required by God. In this way, the student of Christ often focuses on gathering information about the Spirit of God, about the Scriptures, and is able to discover *some* applications in real life. A disciple of Christ seeks to perfect the skill of *seeking out* life and character changes each time the Spirit is speaking to him.

While much of the New Testament specifies how we are to live, the struggle of knowing what God wants us to do deals with the options we consider and do not consider during our own unique and uncomfortable life situations. And, while *all* the principles of living for Christ are specified in the New Testament, the Scriptures are silent on many *specific* applications. Those silent areas are areas of concern. Those silent areas are the ones that keep the task of knowing God's will in every situation from being decidedly easy. Those silent areas are the ones which, if we cannot hear the Spirit consistently and clearly, we will tend to develop huge chains of logic in our attempts to make the silent areas black or white — like the Mosaic Law.

Using logic to figure out the silent areas of the Scriptures can inadvertently minimize actual need to listen to the Spirit of God with the heart for some believers. This is because logic does provide answers, which may be correct sometimes, but may also be incorrect at other times. Leaning on our logic can cause us to believe that the logic itself is consistently of the Spirit and is the way we "hear" the Spirit provide His counsel. Viewing logic in this way seriously underestimates Satan's ability to influence our thoughts, motives, desires, impulses, attitudes, interests, preferences, etc.

In saying that logic is not a substitute for hearing the Spirit's voice within, it is important not to assume this means we are supposed to be unthinking, mindless idiots. While logic itself is not bad or useless, substituting it for the voice of the Spirit can come dangerously close to leaning on our own understanding. Logic must never be elevated to the position God gave our hearts (1 John 3:18-24). The disciple of Christ learns to observe and appreciate God's design in the dynamics of the heart and mind in order to achieve a godly balance between the two; this does not come naturally to us.

The differences between student and disciple can be seen in some of the differences between learning in school and learning in discipleship. In school, how, why, and when the students complete the assignment is not something which is often tied to the student's evaluation. This is not always true in discipleship beyond the elementary teachings of Christ. The Spirit hears what is in the heart and speaks to what He hears (John 16:12-13). In school, *when* a student works on an assignment, and even the nature of the assignment itself, may or may not affect the student's life directly. This is never true in discipleship.

In school, teachers have less personal interaction with students, not only in class, but in terms of the student's life experiences after class. This is not the case in discipleship beyond the elementary teachings of Christ. In school, the teacher's intention is to pass on knowledge, information and some hands-on experience. This is not the same in discipleship. In discipleship, a disciple's difficulty in a particular experience reveals the knowledge which must be reviewed in order to clarify the part of the application that must be improved.

In school, procrastination isn't as much an issue as long as the work gets done, even though the quality of the work may not be the highest and best the student is capable of doing. In life, and being discipled beyond the elementary teachings of Christ, procrastination can be viewed as the spiritual opposite of perseverance.

When a disciple learns to hear the Spirit's guidance and is tempted to procrastinate, Satan's tactic is obvious. When Satan is not successful in preventing a disciple from hearing the Spirit's guidance, then Satan's next move is to get him to procrastinate. This scheme of Satan is what often causes disciples of Christ to fall behind in following through with the guidance the Spirit gives. It leads us to sin even though we heard the Lord correctly. Another factor which may cause a disciple to procrastinate and act as Satan wants is the inability to skillfully transform the pain associated with Satan's attacks or the Lord's discipline.

In Genesis 12:2-3, the Lord made some promises to Abraham about where his life path would lead. While the Lord seeks to guide us, He doesn't always promise us a particular outcome in life. Often our life paths differ in this way from biblical figures like Abraham. When cultivated, a disciple's ability to consistently hear the Spirit speaking leads to a series of directives or guidance which, when linked together, lead the disciple along a life path the Lord intends him to follow. In the lives of those whom the Lord *hasn't* promised a specific outcome, like He did Abraham, intermittently hearing the Spirit's guidance or hearing His guidance correctly from time to time changes the Lord's desired path for the disciple.

Just because we act in ways other than how the Lord would have us act, this doesn't mean that the Lord's purposes and plan in general is thwarted. It simply means the path that comes with a greater consistency of hearing the Spirit's voice is a path that is consistently greater in glorifying the Lord. The question is how much do we want our lives to glorify God? If we intermittently act in ways other than how the Spirit is guiding us, then God is not being glorified by our heart in those moments; the old self and Satan are! The consequences associated with those sinful actions affect us on our path. As the time in one's life ticks past, the more we procrastinate, the more we give away our own opportunities to glorify the Lord in the powerful ways He offers those who love and serve Him. While the Spirit speaks when we need to change, being discipled is what helps us routinely hear His guidance and counsel.

Students of Christ may know about the meaning of spiritual procrastination, but in real-life situations, they do not see them well. This is because a student of Christ sees the fulfillment of discipleship as gaining information about God and hearing the Spirit's voice, when doing so is easy and seems to come naturally to him. A disciple of Christ recognizes the significance, the blessing, and the challenge of being able to interact with the Spirit on a consistent basis, knowing that when it isn't easy, Satan is definitely attacking. As such, the disciple treats disturbances in the heart, regardless of how mild or painful, as being of an urgent spiritual nature for himself.

Students and disciples have very different attitudes toward learning. **Generally speaking, the student view is "teach me what I need to know, but I don't *need* you to know how I live or what I do with the information I learn."** This view is not what we are to have if we *actually* recognize our own need for discipleship beyond elementary teachings.

If a believer does not recognize a need to be discipled beyond the elementary teachings of Christ, then that believer will find no usefulness in participating in discipleship from a human teacher or in a fellowship with believers that focuses on learning to hear the Spirit skillfully. It is best not to try to coax a believer into being discipled beyond the elementary teachings.

If a believer says he has the need to be discipled but chooses to remain staunch in keeping his application situations to himself, then the believer's participation will be counterproductive for all involved in the discipleship environment. When a believer holds such views, he or she is essentially claiming the ability to identify when and where Satan is attacking and what the Lord's discipline is. The believer is in essence claiming the ability to consistently hear the Spirit one-on-one. That is OK. But if that is the case, the need for the two discipleship environments involving believers has already been fulfilled.

We discussed that the Lord teaches by giving us practical application opportunities through His discipline. The disciple brings these to the human teacher regularly, and the human teacher *assists* the disciple in hearing God's voice, as necessary, and provides guidance and suggestions (sometimes strongly too). Regardless, the disciple listens to God for himself and does whatever he believes he must. The difference between a student and disciple is that the disciple has the courage and interest to examine his own painful, non-pleasant experiences with other believers. The student usually wants painful discipline to hurry up and end, and embarrassment prevents the student from examining recent difficulties or failures with other believers. Further training in the elementary teachings may help the believer to see his own need to go beyond those and to learn to listen and interact with the Spirit consistently.

When we believe being a disciple is like being a student, believers may consider the feeling aspect of our humanity to be about weakness. That view of painful experiences causes us to do whatever it takes to avoid pain we cannot "control, manage, or relieve." In the process, we quench the very voice within that can teach us how to transform that pain. Those who believe being a disciple is like being a student will either struggle frequently in transforming pain to peace, will become skilled in stuffing emotions and venting, or will become skilled in distracting themselves from inner conflict in an attempt to feel peaceful. When we live like students of Christ instead of disciples of Christ, the "transformation" of fears and concerns into "peace" will hinge on how much time has gone by (to wear away painful memories), whether or not a painful situation turns in our favor, or whether we can accept a painful situation as being out of our hands.

When we believe being disciples is about being good students, distraction and entertainment can begin to play key roles in our lives as important *coping* mechanisms for dealing with emotionally painful experiences associated with the changes the Lord is asking us to make. Students of the Lord are not as skilled at transforming painful experiences which actually involve the Lord's discipline. Students of Christ may mistakenly use Scriptures to justify many desires they have in life without being consistent in determining whether the Spirit is speaking to change in some of those desires. Students of Christ will feel good about doing so because the Scriptures are God's written Word. They believe that because they have the desire, and because they love the Lord, their desire must be of God.

Students of the Lord often focus on helping everyone else to the point that they fail to routinely and thoroughly examine their own lives in the way disciples will. The changes God wants in them are things they think the Lord already accomplished mostly in the past. To students of Christ, continual change in their lives is equated almost solely to the ability to be grateful for how He changed them in the past. Students of Christ often believe they have already made most of the changes God wants them to make. They will feel good until someone hints that they might be missing something. This happens in believers when Satan influences them and keeps them from coupling their Scriptural knowledge with a close examination of themselves. Regular and skilled self-examination with the Spirit is part of being able to offer acceptable service to the Lord!

When we believe being disciples is about being good students, we will read God's written Word to learn how others lived for God. But when we believe being disciples is about being good students, we will not really realize why we don't routinely experience the same kinds of personal interactions with God we often see demonstrated in the lives of those whose stories we read. We will come to think we don't have similar experiences because God has changed how He works since biblical times. The truth that it is us who *aren't* changing according to the Spirit's counsel often conflicts with the fact that we have good intentions and consciously desire to follow His counsel. Students of Christ usually do not realize that our good intentions cannot precipitate change in our hearts when Satan is attacking and influencing us, unless we interact with the Spirit skillfully. Good intentions to follow the Spirit's guidance are not necessarily a substitute or reflection of good interactions with the Spirit.

Students of Christ know there are many things God wants to do for us, with us, and among us, but how those things happen will be the question that programs and events are thought to answer. Students of Christ might even debate back and forth on how to make those things happen because it is difficult for them to hear the Spirit leading in the way that will bring unity and harmony in the body. When we believe being disciples is about being good students, we will emphasize *the acquisition* of a personal relationship with God, even among believers of many years. These things limit our awareness of the spiritual war within and diminish our ability to be victorious in our daily walk with the Lord.

The differences between a student of Christ and a disciple of Christ can be summed up by the following:

The student of Christ focuses primarily on learning, while believing that Scriptural knowledge itself is what permits the Spirit to change the heart. **The disciple uses Scriptural knowledge to learn to focus primarily on the condition of his heart, believing it is with the heart that we interact with the Spirit and change.**

How Is Being Discipled by the Human Teacher Different from Being Mentored?

There are differences between mentorship and discipleship. The same is also true for "personal coaches," and "life teachers." This discussion applies to each of these kinds of distinctions. Still, perhaps the closest likenesses to discipleship in the Western world today are often those sorts of relationships.

A person who is mentored may be closer to being discipled than the average student today, provided the mentoring is founded on the elementary teachings of Christ. The most significant differences between mentorship and discipleship are: the mentee's commitment level upfront, the roles between mentor and mentee as opposed to the roles between teacher and disciple.

A person's *willingness* to learn in a mentorship scenario is limited by a number of factors, **nearly all of which introduce old self-interest as a factor:**

1. Whether the mentor is the mentee's boss.
2. Whether the mentee likes the lessons.
3. Whether the ego, sense of pride, and the old self will be permitted, by the mentee, to limit the mentee's willingness to learn.
4. How closely the lessons relate to private, personal life.
5. The mentee's ability to trust.
6. How much, in order to even think about certain aspects of self-evaluation, the mentee requires personal comfort.
7. How much control the mentee feels he or she needs.

It is true that these same factors can become issues between the human teacher and disciple. The Scriptures indicate that some of those factors actually did surface in the discipleship environments. However, when they do surface in a human teacher/disciple relationship, the human teacher will speak directly to them. In some situations concerning the above factors, the cost of changing may be too high for the disciple and may bring about an end to the human teacher/disciple relationship.

In contrast, mentorship is often bounded by some structure that makes it inappropriate for some of the above issues to be addressed openly or explicitly. In discipleship with a human teacher, those issues will be addressed when and where they relate to the disciple's spiritual growth lessons. The human teacher/disciple relationship is expected to identify issues and work to support the disciple in discovering how and where he needs to grow and adjust, regardless of where in life those opportunities are. Reasonable time, support and encouragement are given for a disciple to adjust to the personal relationship with the human teacher, but taking time to grow comfortable with the human teacher/disciple relationship cannot turn into a lifelong adjustment period, if the relationship is to be useful and serve its purpose.

When the above seven factors are addressed directly by a human teacher, it is completely appropriate. This is because the commitment between human teacher and disciple involves real-life application and any life issue may potentially be discussed. It is expected that the motives and concerns associated with discipleship will be assessed by the disciple upfront. Recognizing that many believers have come to hold other kinds of views of discipleship, the human teacher can help a disciple see what must be assessed. A believer's self-assessment prior to being discipled beyond the elementary teachings includes helping the disciple to have a solid idea of how strongly the human teacher will challenge the disciple to grow.

What Is the Difference Between Christian Counseling and the Human Teacher/Disciple Relationship?

This is an excellent question as some of the tasks of discipleship and the personal nature of the human teacher/disciple relationship are similar to those seen in Christian Counseling.

This is because the need for Christian Counseling is related to our need for discipleship! As Christian Counselors would no doubt point out, it is no coincidence that the Spirit of God is called "The Counselor" (John 14:26). Some of the differences between the two are:

1. Discipleship with a human teacher is for any believer who seeks to go beyond the elementary teachings of Christ and become skillful in the real-life application of God's Truth.

2. The spiritually intimate, personal relationship between the human teacher and disciple of Christ permits discussions and provides assistance other than just at regularly scheduled times.

3. The accessibility of the human teacher and disciple to one another.

4. Any of the disciples might be trained to become human teachers.

Often a time of crisis or a specific life issue is the condition under which Christian Counseling is sought. This is not always true for discipleship. Discipleship is for all believers. Many disciples may have difficult personal problems or challenges, and resolving them may be part of the disciple's motivation to seek out the human teacher. But discipleship fundamentally deals with learning how to open one's heart regularly, how to become aware of spiritually intended conflicts, and how to problem solve with the Spirit in normal real-life situations. It deals with developing the believer's experience of God in life situations when the old self is active. As such, believers may seek to be discipled even though from someone else's point of view it seems as though their life is just fine. While discipleship can assist believers in crisis, it is ideal for those who seek training and skill in listening to the Spirit of the Lord before a crisis of some sort arises in life.

The human teacher and disciples may have the kind of spiritually intimate, personal relationship that comes from being part of each other's lives in much the same way good friends interact with each other. The human teacher and disciples can spend time together and seek to develop personal bonds in a relationship extending beyond the times when the teacher helps the disciple with his spiritual lessons (lessons of the Spirit). They seek to cultivate spiritual family bonds like those of a healthy biological family that lives close together.

The human teacher may contact or visit the disciple and vice versa. A disciple may wish to get together during the day or in the evening to discuss and examine some current issue. This isn't always the case in Christian Counseling. The human teacher may suggest they get together based on some recent development in the disciple's situation. The interactions may take place in person or over the phone. They may meet in the believer's home or in some other quiet and private place.

There are times when disciples get together one-on-one or in small groups with the human teacher. There may be regular times when the human teacher and disciples meet together, but those are not the only times they meet during the week. The human teacher and disciples may meet together socially or to work together in accomplishing some service for others. While the teacher and disciples may be together for reasons other than discipleship, when the need arises, the interactions can immediately switch to focusing on hearing The Teacher (the Spirit) and relating in the roles defined by the discipleship relationship. The human teacher and disciples are not necessarily meeting on a professional basis or as part of the human teacher's means of earning an income. They are part of each other's lives and don't necessarily have to schedule time in order to see one another.

Disciples learn that even when the human teacher is assisting one disciple, this normally doesn't mean other disciples may not join in on the interaction. Teaching and learning that profits one disciple can easily profit others. Discipleship capitalizes on that opportunity. Of course, the trust and maturity levels of the disciples do take some initial time to come to a place where they are comfortable with these interactions, but this is a goal which is identified upfront and continually developed.

The teacher/disciple relationship isn't just about the disciple receiving help from the Spirit and the human teacher. Part of a disciple's training involves learning how to support others in listening to God by observing the human teacher working with another disciple. At other times it involves practicing helping one another under the watch of the human teacher — when it is appropriate for all those involved. In the beginning, the disciple learns how to listen to the Spirit and apply certain Scriptural principles to his own life. As the disciple becomes skilled at that, the emphasis for that disciple shifts to prepare him to become a human teacher, provided that is God's will for the disciple.

These differences between the teacher/disciple relationship and Christian Counseling must NOT be understood to imply that Christian Counseling is inappropriate or that its place in building up believers in their relationship with God isn't needed.

HOW DOES PREACHING RELATE TO THE HUMAN TEACHER'S TEACHING ROLE?

Today, preaching is often considered the primary teaching role in churches, and other roles are subordinate. Preaching the gospel is part of the elementary teaching, and it is not the fulfillment of discipling believers beyond the elementary

A Disciple's Heart

teachings, which requires an intimate, two-way interaction.

There are two purposes for preaching: evangelism and edification. Preaching to lead to "making" disciples of Christ (leading others to Christ) is evangelism (Ephesians 4:11; 2 Timothy 4:5). Preaching for edification is teaching that applies to all the listeners. This is different from the specific application assistance and training received in discipleship. Still, while preaching is not a substitute for discipleship, it may be part of it.

It is easy to come to think that because a believer is preaching, the believer has been or is being discipled in one of the three discipleship environments. In this way, preaching may become viewed as an indicator or qualification. You may not be able to make a determination concerning someone's ability to be discipled or to disciple others by evaluating preaching alone. This is because preaching is usually informational in nature. Preaching does not normally contain the two-way, spiritually intimate interactions demonstrated in discipleship itself. Many who deliver sermons and messages are not willing to field personal, real-life application issues, which is part of discipleship. Increasingly, the opportunity to disciple is shifting away from the church body itself. It is, however, appropriate and responsible that some preachers do not seek to disciple believers if for some reason they are not able or available to disciple. This doesn't mean those preachers are ineffective or not needed.

Preaching may be the "public open door" aspect of a human teacher's ministry. A preacher may be the teacher for some individual disciples, or the preacher may not have any disciples of Christ whom he personally watches over and teaches beyond the elementary teachings of Christ. People who are being discipled by a human teacher may, on the other hand, be among those receiving someone else's preaching. Discipleship is defined not by preaching itself but by the personal and spiritually intimate interactions the human teacher and disciple frequently have, which focus on hearing the Spirit in the heart.

Hearing someone's preaching is not what makes the listener a disciple. In the case of evangelism, receiving someone's preaching is a tool God uses to try to speak to the listener in a way where he may choose to be discipled. In this way, evangelism serves as an introduction to living as a disciple of Christ and ultimately points to going beyond the elementary teachings.

In the case of edification, receiving someone's preaching is often inadvertently reduced to information when the listeners themselves are not actively being discipled beyond the elementary teachings. That happens when the listeners do not recognize a personal need for assistance in opening their hearts and are not prompted to ask to be discipled beyond the elementary teachings. When the listeners *are* aware they have unmet spiritual needs, often the need is not strong enough to motivate the listeners to be willing to openly examine their own application skills. Sometimes the listeners simply do not understand what being discipled beyond the elementary teachings will do for them, their lives, and their relationship with God.

WHAT IS INVOLVED IN RECOGNIZING A HUMAN TEACHER CAPABLE OF DISCIPLING OTHERS BEYOND THE ELEMENTARY TEACHINGS OF CHRIST?

It is important to realize that the human teacher/disciple relationship involves *two* people who are not separate but rather *in relationship*. Therefore, when looking for a human teacher, the ability to recognize a human teacher is influenced by certain dynamics within oneself. Recognizing the human teacher is

A Disciple's Heart

NOT *just* about the teacher. Remember, disciples will experience human teachers differently.

When we try to recognize such a human teacher, our tendency is to predetermine the characteristics of the teacher. The way we predetermine the characteristics of the human teacher, in a potentially erroneous way, is to do so without skillfully evaluating the sinful patterns of our own lives. Without evaluating ourselves skillfully, we may not see how the spiritual war unfolds uniquely within us. This means that our own sinful patterns can influence what we seek in a human teacher (2 Timothy 4:3). When we predetermine the human teacher's characteristics in that way, it is based on **our perceptions of what we need, what we *think* we need to be taught, and/or whether we think receiving the teaching itself is the same as living for God.** These tendencies have significant implications.

When we predetermine the attributes of the teacher without evaluating ourselves, that action mirrors the deeper desires of what we selfishly want to become. It can cause us to have imaginings that the application of the teaching is something we, including our old selves, will usually enjoy! We can recognize that some of the recipients of biblical letters accepted the tough life applications the writers wrote about. They were often pleased in whatever costs were associated with being disciples of Christ and living for Him. The recipients were able to do so because they had understood, recognized, and accepted the reality of their need.

The extent to which we determine our own needs and desires, and then accept them whether or not we have evaluated them, influences what we hear when we are being taught. Read that again. If we minimize what we consider to be our spiritual needs, we permit our old selves to exert a certain unconscious desire. That unconscious desire can cause us to believe that we live better than we actually are living. That unconscious desire causes us to exert a control in the form of what we think we need to learn. In other words, if our self-assessments do not accurately reflect what our lives reveal, we must improve, then we are not being honest with ourselves. When that happens in a believer, he will reject being taught beyond the elementary teachings. Inaccurate assessments of our needs, conscious or not, lead us to create unfounded expectations for how spiritual teachings should affect us and why. That influences what we seek in a human teacher.

When a human teacher might challenge us personally in terms of real-life application, we sometimes don't question ourselves as much as we actually question the teacher; this is normal in spiritual war. When we try to understand how to recognize a human teacher, we tend to view ourselves as the believers of Ephesus, who were doing fairly well. We typically do not view ourselves as being like the believers of Corinth, who were doing poorly. This is because our sins often look different, and we don't always see our sins as clearly.

Our views of ourselves influence what we look for in a human teacher, especially given that we have the ability to choose any teacher with any style we desire. Recognizing and evaluating the spiritual quality of our own desires and needs are at the heart of being able to follow the Lord's guidance for evaluating a human teacher. What is in the heart? Who put it there? When seeking or evaluating a human teacher, you need to know the answers to these questions based on what is in your heart.

While God offers help and speaks to all believers, there is a requirement to being discipled beyond the elementary teachings of Christ which is often overlooked. A believer must actually realize that a significant reason being discipled is sometimes challenging, the thing that makes it hard for a believer to effectively hear God's Spirit, the need which the believer seeks to fulfill, lies within the believer himself in various forms. In other words, the human teacher's qualities and abilities must certainly be assessed. But the believer is also a big variable that influences the effectiveness of discipleship. A believer must accurately recognize the nature of his spiritual needs in order to potentially be discipled effectively beyond the elementary teachings of Christ in any of the three discipleship environments, including one-on-one with the Spirit (page 29).

Usually a believer is most aware of his spiritual need to be taught how to live at the time he chooses to follow Christ. The disciple's awareness of his spiritual need to be taught how to live reflects the disciple's awareness of his need to be discipled beyond the elementary teachings. Regardless of when a believer becomes aware of the need to be discipled, the believer is ready to be discipled beyond the elementary teachings when he is aware there is some kind of reoccurring faulty thinking within himself. The believer will know he needs God's specific help in correcting that faulty thinking whenever it arises. This awareness will correspond to a feeling of discontent with any number of the following which the believer is recognizing within himself:

1. Selfish desires.

2. Not sure sometimes how the Lord wants him to submit and change.

3. Not sure of the Lord's disciplines and Satan's attacks in certain real-life events.

4. Not sure what is the Spirit's guidance and counsel in certain real-life events.

5. Not consistent in transforming pain to peace quickly and consistently *without* having to *distract* himself with worldly activities (which is not to say these activities are all bad, but

they can become that way when they are distraction and coping mechanisms for heart disturbances).

6. Uncertainty concerning the Lord's will in some situations.

Essentially, the believer open to being discipled knows he is "sick" and is having difficulty following the Physician's orders (Mark 2:17).

It is wise to evaluate human teachers, determining whether we are being taught correctly versus whether our old selves are misleading us and turning us against our teacher. This is a critical assessment in the spiritual war. This is one reason why we use doctrine as a filter or gauge when assessing other believers. But remember that even with a "proper teacher" there are many times when it will be your old self that causes the problem, not the teacher. It is what happened when Jesus returned to Nazareth (Luke 4:14-30). Initially Paul was in the same boat because of his sinful and violent past (Galatians 1:13-17). Similarly, Timothy's instruction was sometimes, apparently, hard for people to accept because he was younger than they were (1 Timothy 4:11-12).

When we predetermine the nature of the teacher *without* a **true recognition and accurate assessment of our own individual shortcomings**, we may perceive the teacher, whom we need, as a threat (2 Timothy 1:15). Our culture influences us to look at externals. While Scripture says our works will show who we are (James 2:18), we can also mislead ourselves in our self-evaluation (Galatians 3:3; James 1:22-25). Having said that, there are at least four general factors involved in recognizing a human teacher who disciples:

1. An accurate assessment of one's need to learn how to listen to God.

2. An accurate assessment of the cost of living for God, at least according to the Scriptures.

3. An interest in actually doing whatever you hear God ask you to do, realizing faith will be required, especially when things may not seem to be in your favor from a worldly perspective.

4. A willingness to recognize whether the teachings are helping your relationship with the Lord to improve, helping you to know His will for you, and helping you to actually experience peace during trials and undesirable situations.

The Scriptures teach what they teach; following the Lord isn't always easy when, with His Spirit, we fight against our old selves. Due to the nature of our old selves, we are often tempted to find ways to be accepted by the world and to feel comfortable in the world when it comes time to apply those teachings. A teacher, be it The Teacher, the Spirit of God, or a human teacher being used by The Teacher, can help us learn to live for Christ, and it will impact our lives.

The impact teachings have on our lives cause us to assess our needs, including spiritual ones, at various levels. Often we sense our need to learn something when we are experiencing discomfort in life or when we are simply interested in something. This is important when it comes to assessing our spiritual need to be taught how to live for God. Those motivations are quite different than seeking to learn and be discipled in how to live for the Lord based on being motivated mainly by love for the Lord.

When we are motivated to learn to live for the Lord because we are uncomfortable or are experiencing pain, Satan seeks to tempt us to turn from the consistency that being discipled requires. Satan offers us distractions and the means to achieve temporary relief from discomfort. Often when we indulge in distractions we pass by opportunities to learn how to persevere and transform the disturbances in our hearts. When we distract ourselves we may feel better temporarily, but our painful problems eventually return. Our desire to strive to do better in learning to live for God may also return. Regardless, Satan's ability to keep us from being consistent effectively minimizes our ability to be discipled beyond the elementary teachings.

When we are motivated to learn to live for the Lord because studying the Scripture is mentally stimulating or interesting, Satan seeks to turn us from being discipled by attacking us more heavily as we grow in our abilities to apply God's Truth to our lives. In other words, as we work on applying God's Truth to our lives, we may begin to experience more feelings like the ones listed on page 20. When we do experience those feelings, our interest in learning to live for the Lord may wane and become less stimulating in pleasing ways. Satan's goal in this case is to use our limited abilities to transform pain to peace to discourage us from improving our transformation skills. Satan may discourage us from learning the transformation skill because we don't like the idea that learning how to transform discomfort requires that we pay attention to and embrace experiences of discomfort.

Let's look closer at how we typically seek to fulfill our needs. As we do, keep in mind that the need to learn to live for the Lord based on discomfort or interest can sometimes be selfishly motivated. The idea is to examine our hearts, to cultivate love for the Lord, and to have our love for the Lord as our motivation for seeking to be discipled. Only a deep love for God will help us persevere through Satan's attacks when we seek to be discipled beyond the elementary teachings of Christ.

When, for example, our need to learn something is at a relatively low level, we may not be willing to change our daily schedules to attend a class. We may purchase a CD or video and learn at home. We may use the Internet to learn while sitting in our pajamas, or we may call an 800 number for customer assistance. It takes time to learn things, and based on our priorities, **changes required to learn can be deemed unacceptable to us.** When learning is at its lowest levels, technology and wealth provide us with services to help us fulfill our needs and to ensure the changes we experience are changes which are *agreeable* to us. These things aren't inherently bad; they simply reflect some of what is important to us.

When the need to learn is at a medium level, we go to school. It is true that sometimes we go to school (where the teachers are) for other reasons: prestige, status, potential job opportunity, etc. But when we are willing to *seek* a teacher, it is usually because we actually want to learn something. If we want to learn about the stars, the solar system, and the nature of things beyond our planet, we find an astronomy teacher. When we want to learn about chemicals, how they work, what they can do, we find a chemistry teacher. When we want to learn about the Bible, the people, the history, the cultures, we find a Bible teacher.

Sometimes when our desire to learn how to live for Christ is at a low or medium level, we inadvertently come to believe that *we* are passionate about something because the person teaching is passionate. In terms of being discipled, we can easily and incorrectly believe we are being discipled because the speaker is speaking and we are excited when listening and thinking about God. In the course of listening to the speaker, some of his/her enthusiasm rubs off on us and we become enthusiastic... temporarily (Luke 8:13).

When a speaker's message leads us to change our lives, our enthusiasm is *not* temporary. While all believers are attacked by Satan and experience times of diminished enthusiasm,

enthusiasm and change is predominant in our lives when we learn how to regularly exercise the skill of transformation in real-life painful events. A speaker's message can't actually facilitate changes in our lives unless we are seeking out the places in our lives where those changes must occur. The main event is NOT about listening to the speaking; *changing* how we live is to be the result of the speaking (James 1:22-25). To experience the difference, the personal interactions and application lessons in discipleship environments become increasingly critical.

When we hear without actually changing, it is because the enthusiasm isn't coming from within us. It is because our desire to learn how to live for Christ is actually at either a low or medium level. Unfortunately, this is prevalent among believers, and it is why leaders in the church are so concerned about the health and vitality of the Body as a whole.

When the need to learn is at its highest level, passion and hunger are involved — your heart is involved! Commitment corresponds to a love from within! When you are really passionate to learn something, the best teacher may very well be the professor in a university, or the professional. But this isn't always the case.

When our passion is high, we seek a teacher who is also passionate, experienced, willing to teach, and who is able to spend time with us. We seek a special kind of relationship because the general teaching provided to large groups of people has been inadequate to meet the application needs we seek to fulfill. We seek the passion and care from someone who can focus on specific needs and application.

When our heart's desire causes us to learn to live for Christ and listen to His Spirit, nothing else is permitted to interfere with the fulfillment of that love, then our need to learn is at the highest level. This is vital to recognizing a human teacher. It comes not just with a love for Christ, but with a conviction that "I must change daily because I love Him!" This comes with the awareness that "my need to learn is great," and because that need is not being fulfilled, "I am failing Him, and that is unacceptable to me!" This is the requisite beginning for any discipleship environment to be able to help you go beyond the elementary teachings of Christ.

When we choose to learn something because we love that thing before even being able to know it fully, whatever else we may do serves no other purpose than to enable us to focus on that which we love. This is how it is when we truly desire to live for Christ and actually interact with Him.

When you want to live for Christ, you desire to change for Him (Philippians 3:7-11). Everything you do is for the purpose of hearing and obeying His commands specifically to you, not just with words but with the passion and skill of an artist or athlete (Philippians 3:12-14). So among the things to look for in a human teacher is the kind of love-filled artist/athlete that is able to let the hand of God work through his heart and can show you how to let that happen in your own life.

When you want a human teacher to disciple you, you find a person who spends time studying his own mistakes, and potential mistakes, regularly (Romans 7:15-21; 1 John 4:1-3). You find a person who has knowledge of what a victory in Christ often looks like because a human teacher has learned and continues to learn to see through the ugliness of mistakes. The human teacher can also see through the ugliness of the consequences of mistakes in order to value the beauty of a person who is learning to interact with God (Galatians 1:13-17). You find a person who recognizes the spiritual value of the most seemingly insignificant spiritual moments (Colossians 3:17) because the little moments are the keys to the bigger ones.

When you want a personal interaction with God and a human teacher who can teach how to develop that, you find someone who spends time seeing how he tunes out the voice of God and uses that experience to learn better how to tune into the voice of God (Romans 7:14-24). When you want to find a teacher who can teach you how to feel God's presence everywhere you go, regardless of what you are doing, then you find someone who sees God everywhere, walks with Him constantly, sees everything as important, and who invites you do the same as a close friend (John 14:23). When you want to find a person who can teach how to have God's will permeate everything you do, you find someone who is willing to know the stuff going on in your life no matter how trying. You find someone who insists that it is all relevant, insists on discussing it with you, and insists you don't hold back (1 Corinthians 3:1-3; Galatians 6:6).

When you want to find a human teacher who can help you learn how God wants you to change, you find someone who can help you follow the Spirit's lead in identifying the patterns in Satan's attacks on you, so you can change those worldly patterns (Romans 12:1-2; Galatians 5:16-24). You find a teacher who rejoices with you in the sacrifices God asks of you and who also can demonstrate how to transform the associated sorrows of your old self (Philippians 2:12-18; Hebrews 12:11). You seek someone who doesn't give glossy overviews but gets to the nitty-gritty of daily life, particularly the life you are most concerned about fixing — yours.

When you want to find a person who teaches how to experience peace and love, you find a person who can show you how to resolve conflicts within yourself and conflicts you have with others while you are in the midst of them, not after the fact (Romans 5:3-5). You will find a teacher who will point out the differences in peace and distraction often at exactly the time they are going on in your life. When you want to find a human teacher who can help you walk with Christ, you find a person who insists you walk alongside him so the application of peace ruling your heart can be demonstrated and not just talked about (Colossians 3:15).

When you want to find a teacher who teaches how to feel the presence of Christ and to live for Christ, you find a person who will not make your decisions for you (1 Thessalonians 5:19-22). You find a person who insists you take responsibility for your own life yet is simultaneously willing to hold your feet to the fire (Galatians 2:11-14).

A human teacher will ask many questions:

- Have you listened to God?
- What was Satan's attack on you?
- What changes does the Spirit want in you?
- How have you been avoiding that?
- Do you need help to work on being at peace with that?
- Has He talked to you about this change before?
- Is your concept of His plan for you in this situation consistent with what He already told you to do when you heard Him in the past?
- What details did He give you to act on?
- What does He want you to say, do, ask, etc. and why?
- What will Satan try to get you to do instead of following through with the Lord's plan for you?

When you want to be taught how to pay attention to Satan's hand in influencing your behaviors, you will find a teacher who will interject Scriptural concepts to help evaluate mistakes often made, even *when* they are being made, and your old self's feathers might get ruffled (Galatians 3:12-14)!

If you have the passionate heart, and it is God's will you be discipled with a human teacher, you will find the human teacher.

WHAT ARE SOME OTHER CHARACTERISTICS OF THE HUMAN TEACHER WHO DISCIPLES?

We mentioned that it is tough to say exactly how *you* might experience a human teacher because both the human teacher *and* you are factors. For this reason, the Scriptures present many characteristics of godly men and women, believers who hold various positions within the church body, and capable human teachers. Some passages actually list some of those characteristics. However, those lists do not provide the only characteristics. Because the Scriptures often demonstrate how to live for the Lord, there are other characteristics we can also use to identify sound human teachers.

The following are a few ways to identify whether someone with Scriptural knowledge is living by hearing and following the guidance and counsel of the Spirit of God. The following characteristics are certainly not guaranteed to protect you from false teachers, but they can be useful in addition to the lists actually provided in Scriptural passages. Remember, old self-deception can make your own judgment questionable, so be careful not to lean on it. Learn to follow the Spirit in your heart; double-check your judgment with God's written Word.

The following are things a human teacher, or a really skilled disciple, who listens to and follows the Holy Spirit **can always tell you** about **himself**:

1. When his last painful experience (temptation) occurred (and

it will often be in the last day or so).

2. What Satan's deception was in terms of "who he is in Christ," and how Satan's deception succeeded against him in his past.

3. How God's Truth about him felt, and how it led to peace *during* the trial.

4. What his misguided motives were (old self's desires). What *changes* the Spirit directed him to make.

5. How he acted in God's Truth about himself.

6. Why his action may not be appropriate for you (why you need to listen to the Spirit of Christ for yourself).

The following are things a human teacher, or really skilled disciple, who listens to and follows the Holy Spirit **will not tell you**:

1. What *the specific attack Satan* is mounting against you is (that is for you to discover by listening to the Spirit).

2. What you or others *should* do in a given situation (other than listening to God to find out).

3. What you or others *shouldn't* do in a given situation (other than listening to God to find out).

4. That you do not have a *direct* connection with God through Jesus Christ.

5. That you cannot directly interact with the Author of the Scriptures, Whom the Father gave us (John 14:26): the Spirit of God.

6. That you cannot choose to have God work through you as He did with the Scriptural saints, disciples, etc. (There is, however, a lot that goes in to such choices!)

7. That Satan has more power than you do in Christ.

8. That experiencing painful and uncomfortable feelings always means you are bad or that you are sinning.

9. That experiencing pleasant feelings always indicate godly living or godly choices and actions.

10. That feeling uncomfortable emotions is a sign of weakness.

11. That being a Christian is just about God.

12. That the only reliable source of Truth is the Bible (that would be contrary to John 16:12-14; Romans 1:18-20; 1 Corinthians 2:6-16; 1 John 2:27-28).

13. That you have nothing to do with the emotional discomforts in your life (Hebrews 12:11; 1 John 3:18-24).

14. That only God is supposed to know why you experience painful emotions (Hebrews 12:11; Revelation 3:19-20).

15. That we do not sometimes feel pain when God is lovingly rebuking us (Hebrews 12:10-11; Revelation 3:19-20).

16. That because and since mankind sinned, experiencing pain or discomfort is God's punishment (Galatians 5:17).

17. That living for Christ is hard only when you are doing it wrong (Hebrews 11).

The following are things a human teacher, or really skilled disciple, who listens to and follows the Holy Spirit, **will consistently do**:

1. Take responsibility for his part in an event which was painful to him.

2. Encourage and support believers in discipleship when they experience heart disturbances. Encourage and support

A Disciple's Heart

believers to listen to the Holy Spirit, to identify how Satan weaves his deceptions against them, and to be consistent.

3. Have love pour from them when they experience painful or uncomfortable feelings. Know how to convert those feelings to peace and love quickly and consistently.

4. Have a great deal of faith in the face of the known and unknown future, but know exactly what the Lord wants him to do in a given situation. Often act very differently than the world does in response to heart-felt issues.

5. Constantly work with the Lord to *change* **himself**.

6. Either desire time alone or to receive support from like-minded believers when a heart disturbance arises, so he can do his part with the Spirit.

7. Encourage others to do the same when their hearts are disturbed.

8. Allow others to make their own choices in order that they may learn to hear and follow God for themselves, yet is willing to give input and support.

9. Experience increasing amounts of peace over time, yet still acknowledge heart disturbances.

10. Regularly be consciously aware of heart disturbances and will admit to and can share the details of Satan's attacks revealed in those disturbances.

11. See God/Truth everywhere.

12. Avoid judging or blaming others.

13. Be willing and interested in talking about the heart of matters in his personal life.

14. Encourage believers to be interested in talking about the heart of matters in their personal lives.

15. Encourage believers to hear the Lord when making tough decisions, and to devote time to learning to listen to God speak to their hearts.

WHAT IF A HUMAN TEACHER ISN'T AVAILABLE AND MY CHURCH BODY DOES NOT HAVE SUCH A DISCIPLESHIP ENVIRONMENT?

This question identifies a problem, but let's be clear that it *doesn't* necessarily mean leaving the church body is the answer.

Many of the New Testament letters show us that when individuals became disciples of Christ, the discipleship that followed was linked directly to the introduction to Christ. In the New Testament, more often than not, when a person was introduced to Christ, discipleship beyond the elementary teachings eventually followed (Hebrews 5:11-12). In being discipled, some believers came to be able to disciple others; they became human teachers capable of assisting others beyond the elementary teachings of Christ. But this was not always the case, at least not immediately. Human teachers would often assist believers by training them in the elementary teachings of Christ and helping them to establish a productive fellowship that facilitated discipleship beyond the elementary teachings but without a human teacher. Then, the "original" human teacher would move on but would often keep in touch with those whom he once discipled personally. Periodically various human teachers would visit to help; particularly when discipleship beyond the elementary teachings was not happening properly (Acts 19:22; 1 Corinthians 4:17).

When you begin to assess your own need to be discipled beyond the elementary teachings, you must determine whether the opportunity is available in the body with which you are associated. This is NOT a call to begin leaving churches and the local Body of Christ just because a suitable human teacher may not be available. However, you must ensure that whatever spiritual needs you have are being met, particularly the opportunity to go beyond the elementary teachings of Christ. This is because the quality of *your* relationship with God and the quality of *your* ability to live for Him depend on that!

If you determine there is no existing discipleship environment which can help you go beyond the elementary teachings of Christ, hopefully you are already seeking the Spirit's counsel on what to do. Remember, while you may recognize a need which isn't being met by the local body, this recognition represents a big battle in your own spiritual war, and Satan will seek to influence you. It would be wise to consider learning more about the dynamics of your own heart and about the principles of listening to the Spirit of God before attempting to make a decision on what God would have you do to fulfill that need. You must examine your life and seek to determine if something in you is resisting the growth opportunities which are actually available to you.

Some believers simply leave a church body when their needs aren't being met. They don't say anything; they simply leave. Treating the Body of Christ in this way is like treating the church as if it is a cable TV provider — when we don't like the service, we simply switch providers. This shows little respect and commitment to the Body of Christ as the Scriptures indicate it is to be treated and interacted with (Ephesians 4:1-3; Colossians 3:12-17).

If your needs aren't being met with the local Body of Christ, consider discussing that with others. Discussing the situation with others doesn't mean just with a couple friends you know from church, but with the church counsel or at one of the regularly scheduled meetings where discussing needs are appropriate. The Body of Christ is supposed to work together, and to respect that the body should have the opportunity to work with you and vice versa.

If your desire is to go beyond the elementary teachings of Christ and to be discipled in the greater application of interacting with the Spirit, seek others who are like-minded. Ask them to join you in taking the issue to the body. But in the final run, if that particular body does not seek to support discipleship, **then you must accept that your situation is quite different from those of the New Testament believers**. If a suitable discipleship environment cannot be cultivated, it is a serious situation, and it is NOT a situation in which Jesus intended believers to find themselves! Consider fellowship for discipleship as an option to take before the body.

If a human teacher is not available, or if, after discussing with the body, the local church body is not able to develop a discipleship environment that can go beyond the elementary teachings of Christ, then seek the Spirit's counsel on getting training to develop a fellowship for discipleship. Again, this should not normally require that you absent the church body.

Chapter 3:

Overview of Fellowship for Discipleship

Growth Step 1:

To recognize the differences in fellowship for discipleship versus other kinds of fellowship we experience.

Growth Step 2:

To appreciate how disciples can give and receive support when learning to listen to the Spirit of God in fellowship for discipleship.

Growth Step 3:

To develop an awareness of Satan's attacks against a fellowship for discipleship.

We have discussed what it means to be a disciple and what it means to go beyond the elementary teachings of Christ. We have examined some characteristics of the human teacher and his role in teaching disciples of Christ how to hear the Spirit with consistency in uncomfortable situations. Let's take a look at how the concepts of being discipled apply to a fellowship of like-minded believers who come together specifically to learn how to listen to the Spirit of God.

To create and participate in a fellowship for discipleship, the foundation must be laid first. The participating believers must

Overview of Fellowship for Discipleship

be familiar with the elementary teachings of Christ. They must have a solid awareness of the essentials for going beyond the elementary teachings of Christ (discussed in Chapter 1); particularly in recognizing their individual needs to be discipled beyond the elementary teachings.

To be clear, in a fellowship for discipleship, each of the believers has some knowledge of the elementary teachings of Christ. Each can acknowledge not having acquired the skill of being able to clearly hear the Spirit speaking on a consistent basis. Each believer in the fellowship can acknowledge the need to learn the "how to" of listening and hearing the Spirit. Each believer understands that acquiring that skill set takes practice and real-life application training, but it is achievable. Each understands that using the skill set is a lifelong effort. In acknowledging these things, we come to the defining characteristic of a fellowship for discipleship. In the fellowship for discipleship, there is *not* the kind of human teacher present that we discussed in the last chapter.

The purpose of this overview of fellowship for discipleship is twofold. First, it seeks to serve as a reminder to believers who are in such fellowship to stay focused on the Spirit of God in their hearts. For believers not in such a fellowship, this chapter seeks to introduce them to the concept of being taught by the unseen Teacher in a fellowship of believers, where it is actually useful to avoid stepping into the teacher role.

Let's clarify one other issue upfront. Some have asked whether fellowship for discipleship is the same as a cell group or a home church. The answer is no. Generally speaking, the purpose of a cell group or home church focuses on facilitating worship. Fellowship for discipleship is not a replacement for regular worship, just like worship is not a replacement for discipleship.

Due to the spiritually intimate nature of the interactions in fellowship for discipleship, it is highly recommended that the fellowship for discipleship group be kept intentionally small. Ten to fifteen believers is about the maximum size for an effective discipleship environment. The minimum size is, of course, two or three (Matthew 18:20). The small size may enable believers who are of like mind, in cell groups or home churches, to easily and comfortably develop the kinds of interactions which are particularly useful in fellowship for discipleship. But any group of believers that is already seeking to cultivate and enhance relationships among themselves will find that doing so lends itself to forming a fellowship for discipleship, provided those relationships go beyond social interactions and strongly include seeking out growth opportunities of the Spirit.

DIFFERENT KINDS OF FELLOWSHIP FOR DIFFERENT PURPOSES

The act of coming together as believers without a human teacher for the purpose of discovering how to let the Spirit guide them as individuals is challenging. The Scriptures indicate that with the Spirit's counsel, believers may support each other in being discipled by the Spirit (Galatians 6:1-2). This should not be thought to exclude continued exposure to the elementary teachings, which may often be received in worship or other church activities.

Fellowship for discipleship is not a task to be undertaken lightly. It requires each believer to continually work to exercise an honest awareness of one's own old self. Just because the fellowship is comprised of believers, that does NOT mean Satan will not attack those believers during the fellowship. Everyone brings an old self to the fellowship, and each believer must pay attention to his own old self.

Today, the idea of fellowshipping together often means that we are doing something with, or in the presence of, other Christians. When we say something along the lines of, "We had some good fellowship time," we usually mean that we connected with other Christians in the course of whatever activity was going on at the time, or maybe we learned something new.

There are times when we fellowship with believers in a classroom setting and the elementary teachings of Christ are discussed. During those times, the discussions may be helpful for removing some of the spiritual blinders over our eyes. We might see some deeper application of God's Truth to our lives. This can even happen in a relatively casual setting with a heart generally open to discussions about God and life.

But those kinds of interactions do not necessarily help us develop the *skill* of clearly hearing the Spirit when He is speaking to us during unpleasant situations. Those kinds of insights and interactions are very different from intentionally being discipled in fellowship with believers without a human teacher. They are not the sum total of learning to listen intentionally and consistently to the voice of God with one's heart during challenging life situations.

The differences between other forms of fellowship and fellowship for discipleship include a skillful study of the patterns in our own lives, interactions that focus us specifically on hearing the Spirit of God, and developing a clear eye to how our old selves are present and seek to assert themselves in life situations.

Fellowship for discipleship is much more than simply getting together and talking about God and sharing the occasional situation you face in your life. It is very different from venting with like-minded believers. Fellowship for discipleship is also greater in scope than just studying God's written Word together. Fellowship for discipleship involves *learning* to see and hear spiritually concerning a specific situation in our lives. It involves *learning* when we cannot see or audibly hear the one teaching (the Spirit of God). It involves learning to listen to the Spirit for specific counsel concerning the kinds of issues we tend to vent about. Fellowship for discipleship involves *learning* with fellow believers without overstepping our bounds in the advice department.

In fellowshipping for discipleship, the importance of interacting as brothers and sisters cannot be overstated. Those of us who grew up in homes with siblings, or who have children, often observe children interact with one another as if they were parents. Children often say things like, "Daddy said not to do that," or "You better not say that," etc. As spiritual children in fellowship for discipleship, these are the behaviors we must NOT imitate, regardless of our good intentions. There is no place for any adult versions of those childish behaviors. In order to participate effectively in a fellowship for discipleship, we must always remember we each have our own need to learn to hear. In order to acknowledge that need and keep focused on it, it is necessary not to take on spiritual parental roles at any time. This is different from what we are used to.

Generally, fellowship for discipleship is not the place for resolving differences with one another (Matthew 5:23-24). While it is important that we resolve our differences, fellowship for discipleship is where we to learn *how* to resolve differences by hearing what the Spirit has to say to us individually when we have differences.

Fellowship for discipleship is not the place for teaching each other. Subtle agendas or suggesting with conviction what someone else should do, good intentions or not, is inappropriate. They are, however, among the easiest behaviors to inadvertently stumble into during a fellowship for discipleship where a human teacher is not present.

The focus in the fellowship is to see and hear the invisible: your heart, the Spirit, Satan. While the purpose of the fellowship is to assist one another to be discipled, the point is to avoid, even momentarily, appointing yourself as the human teacher! Believers learn to support each other directly and "teach" each other indirectly. Fellowship for discipleship is about learning to help others hear the Spirit by getting our old selves out of the way. The same is true among disciples with a human teacher.

The absence of a human teacher from a fellowship for discipleship means it is very helpful for each believer to *have to ask* for another's theological views before it is appropriate for someone to share them with that believer. If someone isn't asking, it is useful to assume they don't want your theological input. It is helpful to agree as a group to give theological input only when it is specifically requested. This places the responsibility on each believer to recognize when he needs help, to ask for it and to decide what he will do with the information. In fellowship for discipleship, it is helpful, and even necessary, to restrain ourselves by not giving ourselves carte blanche permission to share theological views or opinions simply because the desire to share arises. This practice is very helpful in preventing situations where some disciples may "shut down" as a result of the overwhelming convictions of other disciples.

In fellowship for discipleship, it is important for each believer to learn to discern applicable theology by listening to the voice of God **in conjunction with an excellent examination of their own current, real-life situation.** Fellow believers will support and help to double-check one another, but they can do so in different ways which we will discuss shortly.

Believers might ask, "How will we learn from one another if we cannot share freely with one another?" You will share freely. But to fellowship specifically for discipleship, it is very helpful to make some important distinctions in what kinds of things we share. The goal is to shift the emphasis from learning directly from one another by telling each other what to do, to supporting one another, to learn from the Spirit through questions we ask. In fellowship for discipleship, the idea is to learn to develop and share useful questions. Making statements is also very useful, but the point in fellowship is to make relevant statements about yourself when it is appropriate to do so.

Fellowship for discipleship is not the place for theological debate (Titus 3:8-9). But that is what can happen when we forget that the purpose of the fellowship is to learn to listen and hear the Spirit within. One's own sense of "the urgent need to tell somebody something" can be put into place by focusing on actively listening to the Spirit for one's self, coupled with actively listening to the other believer(s). In examining one's own heart, the true motive for making a theological point can be clearly seen. Training, in the dynamics of the heart and mind and the principles governing how to hear the voice of God with the heart, helps greatly in this area.

We often make a point of showing what we know. Fellowship for discipleship is not for showing what we know but learning from the Spirit that which we don't know about how to live well. We have to learn how not to leave the Spirit out of the process.

Confidentiality is critical to building trust among the believers in the fellowship — no gossip (Proverbs 20:19). Gossip is about thinking it is OK to share other people's stories outside of the fellowship without having the expressed permission to do so. We are often tempted to do this anyway because we think we have lots of "good reasons" to do so. Members of the fellowship must agree together how to handle what is shared in the fellowship and avoid doing so in the absence of expressed permission to share. It is very helpful *to have to ask* permission on a case-by-case basis before sharing someone else's story. Even when permission is given, it is useful to minimize that practice.

When we want to share a fellowship member's story outside of the fellowship for discipleship, it is often because their story somehow seems more remarkable than our own. We often share other believers' stories to persuade people to participate in what we are doing, or sometimes just because it makes for "great spiritual testimony." When sharing a story is appropriate, perhaps because someone is inquiring about the fellowship for discipleship, it is best to share your own story. If you are being discipled, then you will be able to share your life's story describing all the issues, pitfalls and dangers you faced due to lacking the ability to listen to God. That should be incredible enough for the storytelling!

SUPPORTING ONE ANOTHER IN RELEVANT, SPIRITUALLY INTIMATE LIFE SHARING

Believers in a fellowship for discipleship focus on supporting each other in a variety of ways. Receiving the support is vital to encouraging one another to share spiritually intimate and relevant information about one's life (Galatians 6:1-5; 1 Thessalonians 5:11; Hebrews 3:13). This means that when believers are absent, they are not available to receive or to give that support. It is most profitable for absenteeism to be limited to the rare exception.

At first, learning to improve one's ability to listen to God's

A Disciple's Heart

voice in the heart is relatively simple. An understanding of how God designed the heart and mind almost immediately enables a believer to capitalize on the principles governing how to hear the Spirit of God speaking in the heart. We are somewhat familiar with that spiritual interaction because we have all heard the Spirit at one point or another, whether we knew exactly what we were doing in our hearts or not. It is quite possible to begin learning to listen to the Spirit on your own and without any real support from fellow believers during the initial stages of learning. This is a lull before Satan's storm.

As you continue learning, Satan will increase his attacks on you in specific ways in certain kinds of situations. How this happens is usually different for different believers. This lasts until after you have shown some serious diligence for a while, then Satan will change his tactics against you to try to create different problems and temptations.

As you learn to interact more regularly with the Spirit, there will come a point when you *will* need the support of believers who understand the personal nature of Satan's attacks and the faith and perseverance required to fight and deny the old self. This need is very real. It is not superficial, nor is it a need that arises out of a mere sense of duty to be part of the Body of Christ. You will *need* the support of like-minded believers who are seeking to interact with the Spirit daily because without them you may find yourself getting lost in the myriad of confusion, fear and/or overwhelming feelings associated with Satan's attacks.

That may sound awful, but it actually isn't. Each time Satan attacks, the Spirit speaks and you can grow if you listen. Just like a tree needs strong roots when the wind blows, in powerful spiritual growth opportunities you need powerful support from like-minded believers in the fellowship. As the tree is buffeted by wind, its roots grow stronger. As believers in fellowship for discipleship increase their abilities to hear the Spirit, the bonds between believers don't just grow deeper and stronger, they become a spiritual lifeline.

How is this so? After the initial stages of learning to hear the voice of God in your heart, being in fellowship for discipleship becomes a big part of supporting you in being honest with yourself and God. Without that kind of support, you will eventually be tempted to negotiate with God when your old self doesn't like His direction. Without that support, you may find yourself struggling to transform painful emotions to peace on a consistent basis. Without that support, Satan will frequently be victorious in tempting you to distract yourself as a means to "feeling better" instead of getting better at the transformation skill the Spirit seeks to guide you in. Without that support, Satan will often be victorious in tempting you to handle life issues and problems in accordance with your old patterns. Fellowship for discipleship has a truly powerful role as a personal support system as you learn how to hear the voice of God.

<u>*James 5:16:*</u> "Therefore, confess your sins to one another, and pray for one another so that you may be healed…"

The idea of sharing our sins with one another implies spiritually intimate life sharing. Confidentiality, trust, and the concept of like-minded believers begin to be seen in a new light.

We may confess our sins when we know what they are, but when we are being deceived by Satan in a given moment, we are not usually aware what the sin really is and how it is playing out in life. This is why the Spirit speaks to guide and counsel us. When we begin learning to hear the Spirit in a fellowship, we learn to recognize when we have sinned and how Satan was able to deceive us. We discover much to take to the Lord in the course of learning to listen in the fellowship. This is not a futile effort, nor is it simply about airing dirty laundry. It helps us to discover patterns in Satan's attacks, and it increases our awareness of when the Spirit is speaking in real-life events. As we develop the skill of hearing the Spirit, we are able to develop the skill of pausing to hear the Spirit before we act in sin!

Confession of sins is for the purpose of reconciling our failures with God and with those whom we offend. This confession is to facilitate change. It reflects discovering the guidance which the Spirit provided to avoid the sin, but which we missed at the time. This understanding is NOT necessarily said to redefine aspects, for example, of various faith groups or denominations (i.e. practices concerning confession). This view is simply provided in the light of the fact that we often examine our sins and temptations to sin when fellowshipping for discipleship.

When we fellowship together to learn how to learn from the Spirit of God with our hearts, we share our listening experiences, and our attempts to listen, with our brothers and sisters. This kind of sharing includes some very specific and detailed information. When applicable, it includes the following:

1. Identifying how and when Satan has deceived us into acting *before* we actually listened to the Spirit's counsel.

2. Identifying what the old self gets or tries to get us to say, do, or believe in during some challenging or difficult situation.

3. Being able to focus on and describe the heart transformation that comes from connecting with the Lord in the heart, and accepting the truth of who you are in Christ.

4. Identifying the change in attitude, motivation, desire, behavior, etc. which the Lord seeks to make in *you* in the situation.

5. Identifying potential courses of action or ways in which you can demonstrate, in the given situation, that you have

accepted the Spirit's counsel and change.

6. Verifying the action(s) you believe the Spirit is guiding you to take by focusing on your heart and changes in it, and the patterns in Satan's attacks.

7. Following through with the action(s) the Spirit directed and paying attention to the results whether they are favorable or not according to the world.

The fellowship helps us to live accountably to God. More specifically, when we recognize times we must listen to God and we don't, this comes out in the fellowship for discipleship. As such, others in the fellowship become aware of the details of the spiritual struggles in our lives. This is a very useful motivation for keeping our eyes on the spiritual ball in our lives. We give others not merely permission to hold us accountable, but the real-life information from our lives which enable others to be in a position to hold us accountable.

In fellowship for discipleship, holding others accountable often happens by asking non-leading, non-loaded questions about one another's "listening to God" experiences. One skill each believer seeks to develop in being discipled is to learn to recognize the Spirit speaking to change within their own heart. But honest self-observation is quite difficult when we aren't very skilled at noticing when the Spirit is speaking to us. When believers do notice and then share and receive support concerning the experience, believers are challenged to discover how to hold *themselves* accountable to the Spirit. This helps facilitate recognizing the Spirit's voice. It helps develop the new self by discovering faults, changes, and ways in which the Spirit wants us to alter our old approaches to life situations. In this way, we can begin to experience spiritual growth by hearing the Spirit instead of relying primarily on the insights, knowledge

A Disciple's Heart

and/or opinions of others in order to discover areas of one's life where the Spirit is speaking to inner change.

The interactions between believers in fellowship for discipleship must be done very carefully and attentively, and the interactions must be based on biblical principles that govern how to listen to the Spirit of God in one's own heart. We mentioned that those interactions include asking questions. What kinds of non-leading questions are we talking about? Below are a few examples. Keep in mind that this is not a detailed discussion about how God designed our hearts to function in order to correctly hear him, so if you read the questions below and nothing miraculous happens, realize they aren't magic questions.[4] The questions below are a small sampling of the kinds of questions that the supporting believers may ask another believer who is in the process of listening to the Spirit of God concerning a specific situation to which the Spirit is speaking.

- What does your old self want?

- What other kinds of situations have you experienced that are like the one you are experiencing now?

- What patterns have you identified in your responses to such situations when Satan is attacking you?

- How does the truth about who you are in Christ feel? Can you set aside the external situation long enough to focus on feeling God's Truth about "who you are in Him" in this moment?

- What change(s) is the Lord seeking to make in you in this situation?

- What value are you being challenged to change in order to live in accordance with who you are in Christ?

---

[4] See the back of the book for more information on the next in the *Series*, which examines those details and the Scriptures which demonstrate them for us.

- What are you afraid of? What are you afraid of losing? What are you afraid will happen or not happen? Are you afraid to ask someone for something (realizing you might not get it)?

- In the situation at hand, what do you need and what do you want? What is the difference between the two? Is "who you are in Christ" requiring you to give up one or the other?

- What might happen in your life if a particular want or desire were not fulfilled? How does being "who you are in Christ" help you to face that potential situation?

- While you are feeling the truth of "who you are in Christ," what ways of handling the situation come to mind, and what options come to mind?

- Do you want to do any of those options because someone else did them to you? Is that what God wants of you in this situation? Are any of your options giving you what your old self wants? What does your old self's pattern show?

- Is the course of action you *think* the Spirit is giving you focused on getting others to cooperate with you, or to change in you what God says you need to change about you?

- Is the course of action causing you to avoid a particular situation or person? Does God want that?

It takes practice and skill to learn to support believers well in hearing the voice of God. A peaceful heart, timing, and attentiveness to the believer are among the keys. Responding to such questions helps us *acknowledge* our spiritual mistakes in a real and useful way. It also helps us learn from our past spiritual mistakes, and to not forget them. It is part of how we emphasize, to ourselves, the need we have to be aware when the Spirit is speaking and what He is saying.

In these ways, especially when the heart dynamics are understood and the principles of hearing the Spirit are grasped, we begin to see it isn't always necessary to tell someone else what God would have them to do. The Spirit can make things clear to us through our hearts if we can become skilled in hearing Him. It starts by recognizing our own individual needs to be discipled by the Spirit in our hearts. When we don't listen well, or when we forget to listen, we will experience the consequences of our choices. This is true whether our choices and actions are based on wisdom of the Spirit, or of the wisdom and desires of the world.

AN OVERVIEW OF SATAN'S WORK AGAINST A FELLOWSHIP FOR DISCIPLESHIP

When believers seek to fellowship together without a human teacher to learn to be discipled and to listen to the Spirit of Christ with one's own heart, there are four key players:

1. The Spirit, Who is The Teacher (He is always present).
2. The individual disciple (you).
3. Other believers who are also seeking to learn.
4. Satan.

As with all situations in life, the role each person fills must be clearly understood and demonstrated not only in one's words but also in actions. While discipleship is possible in the company of other believers, the very presence of other believers can be used by Satan to cause any or all the believers involved to fail to learn to hear the Spirit. Satan typically accomplishes this by diverting our attention from our hearts and leading us to debate one another versus examining our hearts. For this reason, coming together to learn as disciples cannot be done simply by reading and examining God's written Word and then talking and venting about our life problems. It is more helpful to examine God's written Word, to listen to the Author's (Spirit's) spoken word in our hearts, and to examine our lives.

A group of believers who do not have a human teacher, may say, "We will fellowship for discipleship in order to get better at listening to God, and we will do it 'in His name'," (a statement which would refer to Matthew 18:20). But that doesn't mean that the product of that fellowship will actually be what God intends. Saying we will do something in the Lord's name means little unless the dynamics in our hearts reflect doing the activity in our new selves. When Satan attacks us and our old selves seek to assert themselves, if we are not skilled in hearing the Spirit's voice then we will not always change as He directs in order to act in our new selves.

When we seek fellowship for discipleship, doing so recognizes that we lack in our ability to clearly hear the voice of the Spirit. This means we are seeking to learn how to be consistent in working with the Spirit to transform our hearts and be able to do things in the name of Christ! Satan will try to get us to forget or overlook this important point.

It is contradictory to believe it is possible to learn about the application of living for God without Satan's temptations! We are not in the Garden of Eden prior to the fall, or in the new heaven and earth! To apply "living for God" in real life means we have a *need* to apply it *because* Satan is trying to get us to live other than for God! Living for God does NOT eliminate Satan's intimate involvement in real life. Fellowship for discipleship is about real life. The Spirit's guidance is in part about how to live a moment of attack and overcoming Satan. Expect Satan to attack during the fellowship.

Do not think that the fellowship for discipleship experience is about a safe haven from Satan's influence. It is about learning to support each other in listening to the Spirit's voice when Satan is trying to attack individuals, even if it happens in the fellowship! When Satan is attacking you, you must use that experience to become skilled in recognizing your old self.

There is no shame in the fact that our old selves often seek to assert themselves, even in fellowship for discipleship. The goal is for the participants in the fellowship to recognize that those moments are moments of great spiritual opportunity. When Satan attacks in the fellowship, it is an opportunity for the participants to work together as the Body of Christ and assist one another in connecting with the Spirit through the heart. If you feel Satan attack you, the idea is to tell others in the fellowship. Everything must stop in order to support you in that moment in the ways we have been discussing.

Due to Satan's influence, the general *intent* of the fellowship members doesn't determine whether strong disciples of Christ are produced or not. In other words, just because the participants desire to grow doesn't mean they necessarily will grow. Growing requires effort, doing your spiritual work, and interacting in the fellowship. If Satan can keep a believer from doing those things, that believer will not become a strong disciple of Christ regardless of how much the believer says he wants that. How well a given fellowship member shares his own experiences with and listens to and supports others determines the usefulness of the fellowship for that believer. **Again, there are both godly and ungodly ways of doing that.** All discipleship environments require a strong awareness of the old self, its patterns and Satan's schemes and techniques for feeding it.

While fellowshipping, what a believer says and does, or doesn't say and do, matters greatly for that believer. Even more important is *why* a believer is inclined to say or not say something. This means *you* need to be aware of why *you* are speaking or not. It is to *your* spiritual advantage to be aware of what motives are in *your* heart and whether resisting that motive is critical to *your* growth in the Spirit or not! These are among the things a believer will need to be paying attention to during the fellowship.

By always being aware of what is in one's own heart, a believer is able to discover when he is being attacked by Satan. Paying attention to your own heart is often a difficult task when you suddenly have an insight into something. But in fellowship for discipleship, the idea is to seek to apply your insights to *yourself* and to *your own situation first* while staying focused on what is happening in the fellowship at that moment. Remember, the Spirit isn't the only one that can generate insights for you. In these ways, you may avoid using your insights as a means to help or get someone else squared away and miss your own opportunities in the process. Fellowship for discipleship is first and foremost about you figuring out your own walk and then supporting the others as they do the same for themselves.

When the Spirit starts speaking to you, the idea is to let nothing else take precedence over that for you. When the Spirit is speaking to you, that is *your* moment of application; it is *your* present opportunity to grow. It is the opportunity to grow in *that* moment. This is true even if you came to the fellowship to get help on some other opportunity you struggle or have struggled with!

A WORD OF ENCOURAGEMENT

We set out to examine how discipleship is directly related to the purpose of glorifying God by cultivating our individual, personal relationships with Jesus Christ and the Spirit, whom the Father gave us. We have discussed that Satan attacks us in ways we do not normally notice because he is a skilled deceiver. We have discussed that there are many issues, problems, challenges, and tendencies we face in everyday living. We have discussed that the patterns associated with those challenges will continue into our future, when our concepts of discipleship do not involve training, support, and encouragement in how to personally apply God's Truth to our lives.

We have also introduced our need to understand the dynamics of the heart and mind, so that we may know when the Spirit of God is speaking to us. Those dynamics are critical to being able to personally apply the principles which govern how God designed us to hear His Spirit's voice! They are critical because many of the elementary teachings speak to those dynamics and principles. While each of us have correctly used our hearts and applied the principles of hearing the Spirit, we must learn to do that intentionally in order to live well for the Lord consistently. This is the purpose of being discipled beyond the elementary teachings of Christ.

Now, let us seek out how we can learn these things. Let us seek out how we can overcome our fears which make us resistant to trying intentionally to hear the voice of the Spirit within the heart. Let us reconnect practical application training and spiritually intimate personal interactions with discipleship opportunities that come with salvation. Let us also consider how to exercise wisdom in this spiritual venture.

You may come to sense that Satan has somehow been successful in preventing you from being discipled beyond the elementary teachings of Christ. The Lord has a way for that to be changed. But the opportunity to be discipled may not simply fall into your lap. While the Lord has a plan, He is going to require *you* to be willing to make some changes in *your* life in order to be discipled. These changes will require you to demonstrate your trust in Him; following through with those changes will demonstrate your faith in Him. If the Lord lays some changes on your heart, then pay attention. Let your love for the Lord grow within you. Don't try to figure out the outcome (Hebrews 11), don't procrastinate, and don't be deterred from following through with the changes the Lord wants in *you*.

Have faith; cultivate a real-life trust in Him. Remember, faith deals with *knowing* the action God wants you to take even though the future outcome is unseen and the mind, filled with fear, is screaming, "Don't do it!" Our over-thinking is influenced by Satan and is a result of the mind trying to "see" first in order to justify the faith required. In the tough times that come your way, trust with your heart and don't run from the challenges your heart tells you to face. Corroborate what you believe is God's will for you by examining His written Word. Then, follow through with what you believe God told you to do **before you start to over-think.**

Seek support of like-minded believers who understand the challenge of siding with Christ to fight Satan in everyday kinds of experiences. **And verify whether your love for Christ is actually being permitted to draw you closer to Him daily; recognize your old self**. Drawing *you* closer to God is what *your* walk with the Lord as His disciple is to do for you. Expect to have to lean on the Lord when you are hearing His Spirit helping *you* change *you*.

Before seeking discipleship, you are going to have to spend some dedicated one-on-one time with the Lord. Don't fit Him in to life; change your life to fit with Him! Set your intentions to do your best according to who you are in Christ regardless of what that may take! This will be required to determine what the Lord wants you to do next with any degree of accuracy. Examine the

Scriptures we have highlighted in our discussions.

Once you believe you know what the Lord wants you to do, try not to keep going back and forth with Him, seeking to negotiate what He wants based on your fear of how it may turn out. That is never a good practice and results in double-mindedness (James 1:6-8). Commit yourself against riding the fence and know that it is possible to transform all pain to peace; seek to learn that.

Prepare yourself to give up slavery to your old self desires by avoiding the temptation to massage the Spirit's direction into your life in ways that are comfortable for your old self. Assess and test yourself in each moment to ensure you are doing as God *has* told you. If you ever discover you may have strayed from what the Lord has said, even without intending to, re-evaluate *your* priorities. Speak to Him and learn how to hear Him speaking to you. Study God's written Word, but don't continually test the Lord by procrastinating and trying to get Him to change what you hear Him tell you to change when your heart is at peace.

Satan tempts us to integrate the salvation message into our lives with a few changes that at first seem huge. But without the continual changes, those big changes in our past become laurels upon which we rest. Many times this happens without our realizing it. When you see it happening in your life, stop and refocus on Christ.

Don't allow yourself to believe that your ability to follow the Lord can come to a point where there is no longer a cost which must be paid in this world. Don't assume that helping others walk with the Lord is a substitute for doing your best in your walk with Him. Seek to be discipled. Being discipled is about seeking out possibilities in our relationships with Christ and His body of believers by learning to hear and follow the counsel of the Spirit. But always keep in mind our individual rights to make choices in each moment, our individual rights to live life as we choose, our individual abilities to listen to the voice of God, and our individual abilities to be deceived are the things within each of us that influence whether possibilities in Christ become our *own* realities.

May you be able to interact well with the Spirit of peace within you.

REFERENCES

Pagan Christianity?: Exploring the Roots of our Church Practices, Frank Viola and George Barna, Tyndale House Publishers, Inc., 2008

HOLY BIBLE, NEW INTERNATIONAL VERSION®. Copyright © 1973, 1978, 1984 by International Bible Society. Used by permission of Zondervan Publishing House

Coming in spring 2010!
Keys To Understanding Life Series
presents Book 2

Feelings 101: Pain to Peace

A Heart Designed to Hear the Voice of God

www.feelings101.com

The next book in the *Series* provides **textbook material, "hands-on" training, personal evaluation questions and real-life exercises** to help you to *recognize Satan's tactics* against who you are in Christ, and to *discover the practical nature of listening to the Spirit of God with your heart.* To assist you and enhance your skills of interacting with the Spirit, the book includes a practical and functional approach that relates to everyday living. *Feelings 101: Pain to Peace* spotlights two Scriptural keys to being effectively discipled by The Teacher: recognizing the dynamics of your heart and mind, and applying the principle's which govern hearing the Spirit with your heart.

- How can you transform, into peace, the emotional pains and discomforts which are often associated with the Lord's discipline (Hebrews 12:11)?

- How does your old self work to influence how you handle the Spirit's counsel to your heart, and your ability to recognize when He offers it?

- How can you identify the patterns of your old self and how can you develop your ability to see Satan scheming against you in everyday, real life?

- What kinds of life situations involve spiritual issues and choices? How can you discover God's will for you quickly and accurately in those situations?

- How did God design your heart and mind to function so that you can learn to hear His voice with skill and consistency?

- How can you discover the specific changes God seeks to make in your life?

- How can you develop your ability to discern between the voice of the Spirit and the influence of Satan, regardless of where you are or what you are doing?

- How can you know whether your current priorities are the priorities God would have to influence your life and relationships?

- How can you evaluate your ability to recognize your unique patterns relating to temptation, your ability to hear and experience God, and your ability to discover the areas of your life in which you can better follow Christ?

Coming Soon!

Keys To Understanding Life Series

presents Book 3

Feelings 201: Fellowship for Discipleship

Developing Your Heart with Like-Minded Believers

www.feelings201.com

The third book in the *Series* presents a "hands-on" training guide to assist small groups of like-minded believers in creating and experiencing fellowship specifically for the purpose of discipleship. It walks believers through the kinds of interactions that precipitate dynamic fellowship and strong bonds as they work together, and individually, to be discipled by the Spirit of God.

- Build on and enhance your knowledge of the elementary teachings of Christ.

- Build on and enhance your training in how God designed your heart and mind to function and interact.

- Build on and enhance your experiences with the Scriptural principles which govern how you may hear the voice of the Spirit in your heart.

This book addresses the following issues in useful detail:

- What are the roles for believers that fellowship for discipleship without a human teacher?

- How can you strengthen your ability to live God's written

Word in daily life by fellowshipping for discipleship?

- How can you actively seek when and how the Lord would have you improve your walk with Him?

- How can you fine-tune your prayer requests and be sure you make them "in His name"?

- How can you share your real-life experiences in a fellowship in order to profit from support of other like-minded believers?

- How can you listen and interact with believers to encourage each other in developing the spiritual skill of hearing the Spirit's counsel within? How can you assist and challenge others to live for Christ without "stepping on each other's toes"?

- How can you conduct practical exercises that facilitate learning to hear the Spirit and to recognize Satan's influence and the activities of your old self?

More about *Keys To Understanding Life Series*

www.KeysToUnderstandingLife.com

This book is part of the *Keys To Understanding Life Series*. The *Series* focuses on how we may interact with and draw upon the power of the Spirit of God available to us through Christ Jesus in our hearts. (This interaction is different from speaking in tongues.) The Spirit authored the written Word of God, and He uses the divine nature of the Scriptures to speak to our hearts (2 Timothy 2:15-16). The *Series* acknowledges that each of us struggles, or has struggled, to hear the voice of the Spirit clearly in various real-life situations.

The *Series* illuminates how the Scriptures indicate we must do our parts to open our hearts to hear the Spirit within. This is often challenging when, in some life situations, doing so doesn't seem easy or to come naturally. The Scriptures demonstrate how others often heard the voice of God extremely clearly, perhaps even audibly, during challenging situations. The *Series* is tailored to examine how the Scriptures show that we too can, and need, to develop the skill of hearing the counsel of the Spirit of God.

As believers, we are to live as disciples of Christ (Acts 11:26). The Spirit seeks to counsel and teach us. When Jesus ascended, the Father gave believers His Spirit permanently that we might receive the counsel and teaching we need (John 14:26), especially during challenging situations when Satan seeks to influence us to act in untruth (John 16:12-14). Being counseled, guided, and taught by the Spirit is fundamentally about being discipled by the Spirit of Christ and of the Father, which Jesus secured for us. Unfortunately, we can unknowingly and adversely affect our ability to experience a connection with the

Spirit of God (1 Thessalonians 5:19). This affects our ability to live well for the Lord.

Keys To Understanding Life Series recognizes that each of us has the opportunity to be discipled by the Spirit of Christ in our hearts. We can be discipled through real-life events which are often characterized by emotional discomfort, stress and sometimes overwhelming feelings and frustration. Combined with the written Word of God, learning to hear the Spirit speaking to our hearts helps us to always know God's will for us. In learning to interact with the Spirit in everyday kinds of experiences, we learn to draw on His power and experience our connection with our God, who is always with us.

The books in the *Series* seek to assist believers to develop vital spiritual skill sets, to assist believers in recognizing the spiritual aspects of real-life issues and to answer questions such as:

- What part do we play in working with the Spirit to transform pain to peace?

- How can we interact with the Spirit to recognize and resist Satan's attacks, Satan's agendas, and Satan's use of our old selves in real-life events?

- How can we hear the Spirit in our hearts and understand exactly how God would have us handle situations in real life when we have questions for the Lord?

- What does it mean to be discipled beyond the elementary teachings of Christ?

- How can we develop the skill of listening to the Spirit in fellowship for discipleship with other believers?

- How is being discipled supposed to affect and change our lives?

- How can we use the Scriptures to help us raise our

awareness of our need to hear the Spirit of God in everyday kinds of situations?

- How can we make our prayer life more practical and useful and ensure our requests are actually being made "in His name"?

- How do we put the various pieces of the Scriptures together and bring to life the meaning and fulfilling nature of living for God?

- How can we handle conflicts in marriage and dating relationships by integrating the skill of hearing the Spirit's counsel?

- How can we teach children to hear the Spirit of God in their hearts in order to include Him in their problem-solving processes and to deal with their issues?

In general, there is often a large gap between principles presented in books versus how we must apply the truths to our *unique* life situations. **Keys To Understanding Life Series** focuses deliberately on overcoming that challenge. How does the *Series* accomplish these challenges?[5]

1. **A textbook format** is used to walk you through the process of recognizing how relevant Scriptural concepts apply to your unique life experiences.

2. **Key Concepts** highlight and tie together with how God designed our hearts and minds to be able to interact together. God's design applies to all human beings.

3. **Key Words,** which mean one thing to us today and may be different from the original meaning, are examined in their original language.

---

[5] Some features may not be used as extensively, or at all in introductory books.

4. **Scripture References** are provided where the text speaks to Scriptural concepts or facts that you may want to examine for yourself.

5. **Diagrams and Charts** depict spiritual dynamics being discussed and provide example information for the skills you can practice.

6. **Special Considerations** point to potential pitfalls, common obstacles, areas of frequent misunderstanding, challenges to real-life application, and expose the tactics Satan often uses against us.

7. **Worksheet Questions and Exercises** provide the meat of application for the material you read. These features are specifically designed to help you examine your daily application opportunities and capitalize on the unique aspects of your life to which the Spirit may be counseling you. These features walk you through the development of your own spiritual skill sets by using your own real-life situations and experiences.

The *Series* cannot help you draw upon the power of God's written Word or the power of the Spirit within you if you do not participate with the Spirit of the Lord by approaching these opportunities with certain heart-felt attitudes and intentions.

1. The Lord will not change your life if you do not pay attention to the way you are and have been living it. He will not change your life if you are not willing to do things differently. You will be challenged to identify the ways you are actually not incorporating what you believe into how you are actually living. If you want to improve how you live for the Lord, then the first truth to accept is that somehow you are not already doing your best — even though that isn't a conscious intention.

2. You must be willing to recognize and accept responsibility for how you interact or fail to interact with the Scriptures, the Author of those Scriptures, and the people and experiences in your life.

3. When life gets tough, and the Spirit is emphasizing ways in which we must change, we often seek distraction. We often try to soak up good times as long as we can when we have been through troubling times. If and when this temptation arises, it is critical to remain consistent in doing your part in exercising the spiritual skill sets you learn through the *Series* and see demonstrated in the Scriptures.

4. We release mental, emotional, and physical tensions in different ways. We often carry at least a little bit of stress, worry, and concern, even when we have the Spirit of God within us. It is important to restrain yourself from accepting these kinds of conditions and be willing to practice transforming stress, worry, etc., to peace by interacting with the Spirit as often as those feelings arise. The *Series* discusses this Scriptural skill.

5. People make mistakes; that includes you and us (the authors). You cannot follow the Lord's counsel and guidance by disregarding, forgetting, or turning a blind eye to your failures, painful experiences, and mistakes. At the same time, you must be willing to transform ungodly experiences of guilt by interacting with the Spirit within.

6. Most of us probably consider at least some of the experiences we have as being out of our control. Hearing the Spirit of God in your heart hinges on you being willing to give up any control issues He may speak to. In practice, this means when you confirm you've understood what the Spirit is telling you to do in a particular situation; you must follow through with what He tells you. That isn't always easy or comfortable to the old self. If following through with His

will causes you to feel uncomfortable or scared, you must be willing to draw on the transformation skill you learn.

7. If you have reoccurring trouble in a particular area of life, don't assume because you may not have been successful in connecting with the Lord before that it will always be too hard. Overcoming yesterday's failures, experiencing certainty today, and developing a consistent confidence in tomorrow are things the *Series* can help you accomplish. We are not talking about solving the mysteries of the universe here. We are talking about hearing the Spirit's counsel and teaching so we might understand, work through, and eliminate the sense of being ill-prepared for life's surprises and the "gray areas" of life. But you must strive to be consistent in doing your part.

8. Learn to criticize your old self. This is vital to new-self honesty. You must be willing to identify the facts and *feelings* of your life situations as you "fill in the blanks" in the exercises the *Series* provides. If you can't recognize how you feel or identify the desires of your old self, you will continually struggle with hearing the Spirit speak to courses of actions that would only make sense if your heart were focused on your new self. Criticizing your old self involves identifying desires you may have to change.

9. Verify the Scriptures yourself. Many references are provided — check them out. Examine the passages provided with other passages relating to the same concepts. Studying the Scriptures and attending regular worship is a critical part of our service to God.

Keys To Understanding Life Series isn't a collection of new concepts. When we have challenges in life, we sometimes have the right concepts, but we are thrown off due to the unique ways we must apply them to our unique lives! This is where the omnipresent Spirit works to help us. When we discover useful, Scriptural applications by *interacting* with the Spirit of God, old concepts often appear new. The *Series* addresses application issues by introducing our own choices and actions as being critical variables in what we could loosely call "life's equations." When we live according to the divine nature of God's written word, and the word of the Author of those Scriptures within us, our life equations can begin to add up to what the Lord would have it to equal. This is an old concept. If the *Series* ever seems to come across with new concepts, it is only because when we examine the Scriptures in terms of our real-life emotional and intellectual experiences, old concepts can have fresh light shed upon them.

Thank you Lord for the opportunity to receive Your help and guidance in our own lives. Thank You for allowing us to be useful tools in Your hands.

May God bless you, the reader, in all your choices, and may you come to love all aspects and experiences of your life, so that you may come to love the Creator more and live well for Him.

About The Authors

The father and son team combine a variety of experiences, including formal theological education, creating spiritually intimate fellowships and teaching powerful personal transformation skills possible in Christ. From their home in Texas, they help others learn how to enjoy the enriching and interactive life of being a disciple of Christ.

Learn more about the authors by visiting their website: www.KeysToUnderstandingLife.com.